The Apocalypse

BLACKWELL BRIEF HISTORIES OF RELIGION SERIES

This series offers brief, accessible, and lively accounts of key topics within theology and religion. Each volume presents both academic and general readers with a selected history of topics which have had a profound effect on religious and cultural life. The word "history" is, therefore, understood in its broadest cultural and social sense. The volumes are based on serious scholarship but they are written engagingly and in terms readily understood by general readers.

Other topics in the series;

Published

Heaven	Alister E. McGrath
Heresy	G. R. Evans
Islam	Tamara Sonn
Death	Douglas J. Davies
Saints	Lawrence S. Cunningham
Christianity	Carter Lindberg
Dante	Peter S. Hawkins
Spirituality	Philip Sheldrake
Cults and New Religions	Douglas E. Cowan and David G. Bromley
Love	Carter Lindberg
Christian Mission	Dana L. Robert
Christian Ethics	Michael Banner
Jesus	W. Barnes Tatum
Shinto	John Breen and Mark Teeuwen
Paul	Robert Paul Seesengood
Islam 2nd Edition	Tamara Sonn
Apocalypse	Martha Himmelfarb

Forthcoming

The Reformation	Kenneth Appold
Monasticism	Dennis D. Martin
Sufism	Nile Green

The Apocalypse

A Brief History

Martha Himmelfarb

WILEY-BLACKWELL

A John Wiley & Sons, Ltd., Publication

This edition first published 2010
© 2010 Martha Himmelfarb

Blackwell Publishing was acquired by John Wiley & Sons in February 2007. Blackwell's publishing program has been merged with Wiley's global Scientific, Technical, and Medical business to form Wiley-Blackwell.

Registered Office
John Wiley & Sons Ltd, The Atrium, Southern Gate, Chichester, West Sussex, PO19 8SQ, United Kingdom

Editorial Offices
350 Main Street, Malden, MA 02148-5020, USA
9600 Garsington Road, Oxford, OX4 2DQ, UK
The Atrium, Southern Gate, Chichester, West Sussex, PO19 8SQ, UK

For details of our global editorial offices, for customer services, and for information about how to apply for permission to reuse the copyright material in this book please see our website at www.wiley.com/wiley-blackwell.

The right of Martha Himmelfarb to be identified as the author of this work has been asserted in accordance with the Copyright, Designs and Patents Act 1988.

Library of Congress Cataloging-in-Publication Data

Himmelfarb, Martha, 1952–
    The apocalypse : a brief history / Martha Himmelfarb.
        P.   cm. – (Blackwell brief histories of religion series)
    Includes bibliographical references and index.
    ISBN 978-1-4051-1346-5 (hardcover : alk. paper) – ISBN 978-1-4051-1347-2 (pbk. : alk. paper) 1. Apocalyptic literature–History and criticism. I. Title.
    BL501.H55 2010
    220′.046–dc22

                                                    2009030164

A catalogue record for this book is available from the British Library.

Set in 10/12.5pt Meridien by SPi Publisher Services, Pondicherry, India
Printed in Singapore by Ho Printing Singapore Pte Ltd

01   2010

For Steve, Asher, Margaret and Ben-Aviv, Ruth, and Abigail

blessing doubled and redoubled

Contents

Acknowledgments

Quotations of biblical books and 4 Ezra, unless otherwise indicated, are taken from the Revised Standard Version Translation, Revised Standard Version of the Bible, copyright 1952 (2nd edition, 1971) by the Division of Christian Education of the National Council of the Churches of Christ in the United States of America. Used by permission. All rights reserved.

Quotations of all portions of 1 Enoch are taken from George W. E. Nickelsburg and James C. VanderKam, *1 Enoch: A New Translation* (Minneapolis: Fortress Press, 2004). © 2004 by Augsburg Fortress. Reprinted with permission from the publisher.

Quotations of 2 Enoch, the Apocalypse of Abraham, the Apocalypse of Zephaniah (the Anonymous Apocalypse), and the Ascension of Isaiah are taken from H. F. D Sparks, ed., *The Apocryphal Old Testament* (Oxford: Clarendon Press, 1984).

The quotation of the Apocalypse of Peter is taken from Wilhelm Schneemelcher, ed., *New Testament Apocrypha, Revised Edition of the Collection Initiated by Edgar Hennecke*, vol. 2, trans. R. McL. Wilson (Cambridge: James C. Clarke; Louisville, KY: Westminster/John Knox, 1992).

Citations of the hekhalot texts refer to Peter Schäfer with Margarete Schlüter and Hans Georg von Mutius, *Synopse zur Hekhalot-Literatur* (Tübingen: Mohr [Siebeck], 1981). The texts in this source are in Hebrew; translations are my own.

Chronology

Kingdom of Judah

622 BCE	"Finding" and public reading of **Deuteronomy**
586 BCE	Babylonian conquest of Jerusalem, destruction of First Temple; Babylonian Exile begins

Persian Period

539–538 BCE	Cyrus of Persia topples Babylonian empire, issues decree permitting exiled Judeans to return home and rebuild Temple
515 BCE	Second Temple dedicated
458 BCE	Ezra in Jerusalem
445 BCE	Nehemiah in Jerusalem

Hellenistic Period

332 BCE	Alexander the Great conquers Judea **Book of the Watchers** (early third century)
200 BCE	Seleucids take Judea from Ptolemies
167–163 BCE	Persecution of Antiochus and Maccabean Revolt **Daniel**

Judea Independent 152–63 BCE

Roman Period

63 BCE	Pompey takes Jerusalem
	Parables of Enoch (second half of the first century BCE?)
37–34 BCE	Herod the Great
Early 30s CE	John the Baptist, Jesus
	2 Enoch (before the destruction of the Second Temple?)
	Revelation (just before or shortly after the destruction of the Temple)
70 CE	Destruction of the Second Temple
	4 Ezra, 2 Baruch, 3 Baruch, Apocalypse of Abraham (late first/early second century CE)
	Ascension of Isaiah, Apocalypse of Peter (early second century)
132–35 CE	Bar Kokhba revolt

Rome as Christian Empire

313 CE	Edict of Toleration makes Christianity legal
	Apocalypse of Paul (late fourth or early fifth century CE)
614 CE	Persian conquest of Jerusalem
	Sefer Zerubbabel, Sefer Eliyyahu (before the Muslim conquest)
628 CE	Christian rule restored in Jerusalem
638 CE	Muslim conquest
	Apocalypse of Pseudo-Methodius (late seventh century)
	Hekhalot texts (seventh century on?)

Chapter 1

Revelation in the Age
of the Torah

The book of Revelation in the New Testament, which introduces itself as the "*apokalypsis* of Jesus Christ" (Rev. 1:1), was the first work to refer to itself as an apocalypse; indeed, "revelation" derives from the Latin *revelatio*, which is the standard translation for *apokalypsis*. For most people the term "apocalypse" summons up images of the cataclysmic end of the world, images that derive in large part from Revelation. But in Greek the term *apokalypsis* has nothing to do with the end of the world. Its basic meaning is "uncovering," thus, more figuratively, "revelation." The association with eschatology derives not from the meaning of the term but from the content of the book of Revelation and other related works.

In scholarly usage the term "apocalypse" has come to be applied to Jewish and Christian works that share features of form and content with the book of Revelation whether or not the end of the world is their primary interest. Although many of these texts never use the term "apocalypse," they present themselves as revelations to a great hero of the past mediated by an angel. The revelations typically take the form of symbolic visions of history, journeys through the heavens, or some combination of the two. The book of Revelation constitutes an exception to this description because its author writes in his own name, and there are apocalypses that differ from the description in other ways as well, as we shall see. But despite the deviations it is clear that the authors of these works write in consciousness of earlier examples of the genre. The interests characteristic of the corpus include not only the Last Judgment and cataclysmic end of the world but also reward and punishment after death, the heavenly temple, the divine throne room, and astronomical phenomena and other secrets of nature. The earliest of the apocalypses were written by Jews in the Second Temple period. The form was soon taken up by Christians, and Jews and Christians continued to write apocalypses through the Middle Ages. In the modern era the production of apocalypses has come to an end, but popular interest in them, and particularly in their predictions about the end of the world, continues.

The understanding of apocalyptic literature as defined by eschatological interests may derive from the book of Revelation, but it finds confirmation in the book of Daniel, the only apocalypse included in the Hebrew Bible. Until the mid-1970s Daniel, which scholars date to the time of the Maccabean Revolt in the 160s BCE, was believed to be the first apocalypse ever composed. Because they saw Daniel as the foundational work of the apocalyptic genre, scholars felt justified in treating eschatology as crucial to that genre. But in 1976 Józef Milik published several fragmentary manuscripts from the Dead Sea Scrolls that forced a reassessment of this view of the development of the apocalypses. The manuscripts contained portions of the Aramaic originals of most of the works included in 1 Enoch, a collection of five apocalypses attributed to a patriarch mentioned briefly in the book of Genesis (Gen. 5:21–4) that comes down to us in Ethiopic translation. Before the publication of the manuscripts, most scholars dated the earliest of the works collected in 1 Enoch to the middle of the second century BCE, shortly after the composition of Daniel. The manuscripts from the Scrolls make it clear that two of the apocalypses included in 1 Enoch, the Astronomical Book (1 Enoch 72–82) and the Book of the Watchers (1 Enoch 1–36), pre-date Daniel.

Ancient manuscripts are dated by paleography, examination of the style of writing found in the manuscript and comparison to other manuscripts, ideally including dated manuscripts. It is not an exact science, and while experts usually agree on relative dates – which manuscript is earlier and which later – they often differ by half a century or more on specific dates. Milik dated the earliest manuscript of the Astronomical Book to the late third or early second century BCE, and there is no reason to believe that the manuscript is the original of the work it preserves. He placed the earliest manuscript of the Book of the Watchers in the first half of the second century BCE, but argued that the peculiarities of the manuscript suggest that it was copied from a significantly earlier manuscript. Thus Milik believed he could demonstrate that the Astronomical Book should be dated to the third century BCE, making it the most ancient part of 1 Enoch and also the most ancient apocalypse, while the Book of the Watchers, though somewhat later, was probably composed in the late third century and certainly no later than the early second century BCE.

Despite the subjectivity of some Milik's judgments about the manuscripts, there has been widespread scholarly acceptance of his dating of both early Enochic works, and the new dates have had a profound impact on the study of apocalyptic literature. Neither the Astronomical Book nor the Book of the Watchers is particularly interested in eschatology. The Astronomical Book focuses almost exclusively on the courses of the sun and moon and their calendrical implications, while the Book of the Watchers touches on the Last Judgment but devotes more attention to other interests such as the heavenly temple and the secrets of nature and the cosmos. While no later apocalypse shares the narrowly focused interests of the Astronomical Book, the interests of the Book of the Watchers recur in many later apocalypses. Yet until the new dates were established, scholars generally took the interests of the Book of the Watchers as idiosyncratic and marginal in comparison to the interests of Daniel and Revelation.

In the same year that Milik published the Enoch fragments from the Scrolls, Robert Kraft delivered a programmatic paper entitled "The Pseudepigrapha in Christianity" to a scholarly conference The "pseudepigrapha," falsely attributed writings, of Kraft's title were the so-called Old Testament pseudepigrapha, works attributed to heroes of the Hebrew Bible that were not included in the Jewish or Christian canon. Kraft's paper called into question what had been the standard procedure in the study of these texts, the excision of obviously Christian elements on the assumption that they were interpolations. Kraft argued that this mode of operation, intended to retrieve the presumed Jewish originals of the works, failed to take into consideration the well-attested interest among ancient and medieval Christians in heroes of the Hebrew Bible and in Jewish tradition. Furthermore, the determination of what constitutes a Christian addition or alteration is inevitably extremely subjective, and the assumption that the impact of Christian transmitters is confined to additions that can be surgically removed is deeply problematic. Kraft called on scholars to take seriously the form of the text that reaches us and to make the context in which a text is preserved the starting point for exploring the context in which it was composed. The work of the Dutch scholar Marinus de Jonge on the Testaments of the Twelve Patriarchs in the years shortly before Kraft's paper provided an example of the kind of work Kraft called for. De Jonge argued that the Testaments was not, as previous scholarship had assumed, a Jewish work with many Christian interpolations but rather a Christian composition that made use of Jewish traditions. In later publications de Jonge sought to show how the Testaments fit into the second-century Christian environment in which he believed it was composed.

Kraft's program has important implications for the study of the apocalypses, for, with the exception of the book of Daniel and fragments of several Enochic works preserved among the Dead Sea Scrolls, ancient Jewish apocalyptic literature reaches us through Christian channels. The Apocalypse of Abraham, which survives only in Slavonic, is a good example of the kind of apocalypse Kraft's prescriptions apply to. There has been considerable progress in the study of the Slavonic pseudepigrapha in recent years because the end of Communism in eastern Europe has permitted more scholars expert in Slavonic to devote themselves to the study of ancient Judaism and Christianity. Still, basic questions remain unanswered. The manuscripts in which the Apocalypse of Abraham is preserved date from the fourteenth century or later. While its original language may have been Hebrew, it was probably translated into Slavonic from Greek; thus the Slavonic may well be a translation of a translation. Not surprisingly given so many centuries of transmission by Christians, it contains elements that appear to be Christian, although there is no unanimity about what those elements are. Following Kraft's advice, a student of the Apocalypse of Abraham would start not by attempting to remove Christian features of the work but rather by asking what role the work played in Slavonic culture in the fourteenth century. For example, he might explore why so many of the apocalypses preserved in Slavonic – 2 Enoch, 3 Baruch, and the Ascension of Isaiah, in addition to the Apocalypse of Abraham – involve ascent to heaven. A better sense of the cultural setting in which the work is preserved also allows us to see if there are significant aspects of the work that do not fit well in that setting, thus pointing to origin in a different milieu. In the chapters that follow, as I examine the place of the apocalypses in early Judaism and Christianity, I will allude only occasionally to the complexities just discussed. Still, it is important to remember that for several of the apocalypses under discussion there is no clear evidence to connect them to the centuries around the turn of the era but only a series of assumptions and arguments, many of which may well be wrong.

Before offering a brief guide to the contents of this book, let me admit its limitations. My focus in this book is on apocalypses, works that belong to a particular literary genre, rather than on apocalyptic ideas more generally, though many such ideas will enter the discussion. Nor have I set out to offer a complete survey of apocalyptic literature. To begin with, I restrict myself to Jewish and Christian works. I do not discuss prophecies of the defeat of foreign invaders from Hellenistic Egypt or journeys to Hades or other extraterrestrial realms from Greek and Latin literature. I do not consider Middle Persian texts that parallel the apocalypses or Muslim adaptations of the genre. Furthermore, though the corpus of Jewish and Christian apocalypses from the formative period for the genre, the third century BCE through the second century CE, is quite small, consisting of perhaps fifteen works depending on the criteria used to determine inclusion, I do not treat them all. I am even more selective in regard to apocalypses and related works from late antiquity and the Middle Ages. Rather than attempting to touch briefly on all the relevant works, I haven chosen instead to focus on themes that seem to me particularly important and to trace their development over the centuries.

In the second portion of this chapter I offer a sketch of Judaism in the early Second Temple period, focusing on the developments most relevant to the apocalypses. Chapter 2 treats the Book of the Watchers. As already noted, the Book of the Watchers is not concerned primarily with eschatology. It is more interested in knowledge about heaven, the angels, and the natural world revealed to Enoch in the course of an ascent to the heavenly temple and a journey to the ends of the earth. The account of Enoch's ascent is the first such account in ancient Jewish literature, and it has a powerful influence on later apocalypses. Chapter 3 turns to the book of Daniel with its visions of the imminent end of history. I place the formal features of vision and interpretation in their historical and literary context and examine the work's eschatological timetables and the figure of the one like a son of man. Chapter 4 looks at the development of these elements – vision and interpretation, eschatological timetables, and the figure of the one like a son of man – in early Jewish and Christian apocalypses that follow Daniel during the Roman period. The chapter focuses particularly on 4 Ezra, written in the wake of the destruction of the Second Temple in 70 CE, with attention to several other works including the Parables of Enoch (1 Enoch 37–71), 2 Baruch, and the book of Revelation. Chapter 5 follows the development of apocalypses in which ascent to heaven plays a central role in the Roman era, including the Parables of Enoch, 2 Enoch, the Apocalypse of Abraham, Revelation, the Apocalypse of Zephaniah, the Ascension of Isaiah, and 3 Baruch. It analyzes the picture of heaven as temple in these works, the relationship between the visionary and the angels, the fate of the righteous dead, and the attitude toward the secrets of nature revealed to the visionary.

Chapters 6 and 7 move out of the Second Temple and early Christian period into late antiquity. Chapter 6 is concerned with two bodies of literature that are deeply indebted to the more ancient ascent apocalypses, tours of hell and paradise that continued to flourish in the Christian Middle Ages, leaving their mark on Dante, and the hekhalot texts, early Jewish mystical works that describe the ascent of the visionary to stand before the divine throne. Chapter 7 considers the fate of apocalypses focused on the end of history among Jews and Christians in the Byzantine era before and after the Muslim conquest. Especially in the Christian works the influence of the book of Daniel continues to be powerful. Chapter 8 turns to echoes of the apocalyptic tradition in the modern era. Few apocalypses have been written since the dawn of modernity, but movements motivated by an apocalyptic reading of history, often by the book of Daniel itself, played an important role in the later Middle Ages and the early modern period among both Jews and Christians. Nor have such movements disappeared in the intervening centuries. After a brief consideration of a number of such movements, the chapter focuses on the Branch Davidians, a small movement deeply indebted to the book of Daniel that attracted considerable attention because of its disastrous confrontation with American law enforcement in Waco, Texas, in 1993. The book concludes with some brief reflections on the central themes of apocalyptic literature from its beginnings to the present.

* * *

The ancient Israelites established two kingdoms. Israel, the northern kingdom, which was larger and more powerful than Judah in the south, fell to the Assyrians in 722 BCE. Judah lasted a century and a half longer. But in the summer of 586 BCE the Babylonian army that had been laying siege to Jerusalem, Judah's capital, finally entered the city. The soldiers tore down the wall that protected the city and set fire to its major buildings including the Temple of the Lord, the holiest spot in the holy city. Most of the population of Jerusalem was taken off to exile in Babylonia, with only some of the poor permitted to remain in the ruined city. The king of Judah fled the city with some of his men, but he was captured by the Babylonians and made to watch the execution of his sons. Then his captors blinded him and brought him in fetters to Babylon. Thus the failed rebellion brought to an end the two institutions that had stood at the center of the life of the kingdom of Judah for 400 years, the house of David, the dynasty descended from Israel's founding king, and the Temple, the house of the Lord, in which the divine presence was believed to dwell.

In response to these devastating losses some of the Judean exiles gave up on their God, concluding that he was either too weak to protect them or too angry. But others accepted the message that the prophets Jeremiah and Ezekiel had been preaching both before and after the fall of Jerusalem. For them the destruction of the Temple and the deposition of the Davidic king did not mean that God had abandoned his people. Nor were these disasters a sign that the gods of the Babylonians were stronger than the God of Israel. Instead they saw the disasters as the work of the God of Israel himself, the only god, who was punishing his people for idolatry and other sins. Yet, the prophets promised, God would eventually restore the exiles to their land and favor them with peace and prosperity. Jeremiah even put a limit on the length of the exile: after seventy years, the Lord would restore his people to its land.

The opportunity to return to Judah came even sooner than Jeremiah had predicted. By 539 the once mighty Babylonian empire was in decline, threatened by the advance of a new power, Persia. As the Persian king Cyrus marched on Babylon, the anonymous prophet known as Second Isaiah prophesied his success. Cyrus was the Lord's agent for the liberation of the Judeans, though as the prophet had to confess, the great conqueror did not recognize the god who had singled him out for this task. The prophet was not disappointed in his hopes. Upon taking power in Babylon Cyrus issued a decree in 538 permitting the Judean exiles to return to their homeland and rebuild the Temple. Scholars understand Cyrus' gracious behavior toward the exiles as part of a larger Persian policy intended to gain the support of subject peoples. But the prophet did not doubt that Cyrus was inaugurating a new era in which Judah's relationship to the Lord would be repaired and her people would enjoy a more glorious state than ever before.

Despite this prophetic encouragement, many of the offspring of the exiled Judeans were not enthusiastic about the prospect of leaving Babylonia, where they had been born, for a land they had never known, and few chose to return. The initial attempts to resettle the region of Jerusalem and to rebuild the Temple did not go well, and it was not until about 520, with the prophets Haggai and Zechariah urging them on, that the returnees finally began the work of rebuilding in earnest. The new Temple was dedicated in 515, almost exactly seventy years after the first had been destroyed, investing Jeremiah's prophecy of seventy years of punishment with great prestige, as we shall see when we turn to the book of Daniel.

But if one pillar of pre-destruction Judah had been restored, the other had not. The Judeans had exchanged one kind of foreign rule for another, and though the Persians were in many ways more generous than the Babylonians, they were not so generous as to restore kingship to the Judeans. It is true that the first governors the Persians appointed for Yehud, as they called the province around Jerusalem, were descendants of David. But while all the Persian governors of Yehud whose names are known to us were Jews, after those first few none is identifiable as a descendant of David. Perhaps the Persians concluded that it was dangerous to encourage the hopes that rule by a Davidide might raise, even if the Davidide held his office at the pleasure of the Persian government. Thus, by the turn of the sixth to the fifth century it had become clear that the restoration over which the Persians presided was to be only partial: a new Temple replaced the house of the Lord that the Babylonians had destroyed and priests could once again offer sacrifices there, but there was no king descended from David sitting on the throne.

But before the end of the monarchy there had emerged the forerunner of a new institution that would stand alongside the Temple during the Second Temple period: the Torah, the five books of Moses, an authoritative written text containing the founding legends of the Jewish people and the laws by which they were to live to maintain their covenant with the Lord. The traditions contained in the first four books of the Torah had been developed and transmitted orally for centuries. But by the last decades of the seventh century writing was becoming increasingly important in Judah, as can be seen from the books of the prophets Jeremiah and Ezekiel, and in 622 BCE King Josiah read to the assembled people the words of a book calling itself the Torah, teaching, of Moses, that had purportedly been found in the Temple. This book was Deuteronomy, or an early form of it, which now serves as the fifth book of the Torah. It is hard to overstate the importance of this development for the shape of Judaism, in antiquity or today.

The book of Deuteronomy laid out a program of cultic reform. By restricting the sacrificial cult to the Jerusalem Temple and destroying the high places, local cult sites that were difficult for the royal establishment to supervise, the reformers hoped to eliminate the worship of any god or goddess except the Lord. Yet according to Deuteronomy this reform is not an innovation but rather the fulfillment of what Moses had ordained while the Israelites were still traveling through the wilderness. Like the apocalypses' attribution of their revelations to great heroes of the Bible, the attribution to Moses lent authority to the reform.

Josiah's sponsorship of Deuteronomy is remarkable because, in addition to placing the cult under the king's control, it also places significant limits on royal power: he is not to have too many horses or wives or riches. Further,

> When he sits on the throne of his kingdom, he shall write for himself in a book a copy of this law ... and it shall be with him, and he shall read in it all the days of his life, that he may learn to fear the Lord his God ... that he may not turn aside from the commandment, either to the right hand or to the left; so that he may continue long in his kingdom, he and his children, in Israel. (Deut. 17:18–20)

It is clear from the Bible's narratives about the prophet Nathan's rebuke of King David for his adultery with Bathsheba and the murder of her husband, and Elijah's condemnation of Ahab for the appropriation of Naboth's vineyard, that the power of kings in ancient Israel was by no means absolute; it was understood that kings, like their subjects, were bound by the terms of the covenant with the Lord. Deuteronomy takes that understanding a significant step forward by laying out the limits of royal power explicitly and in writing.

Deuteronomy's ability to rein in unwilling monarchs was never really tested. Josiah died in battle against the Egyptians in 609, and less than twenty-five years later the kingdom of Judah came to an end at the hands of the Babylonians. Though it viewed Josiah as the best king ever, the book of Kings does not think highly of his successors, whom it accuses of doing evil in the sight of Lord as their fathers had done, but it tells us far too little to allow us to draw any conclusions about their attitude toward Deuteronomy.

The earliest definitive evidence for the Torah as we know it with its five books is the Greek translation made sometime during the third century BCE. But it seems likely that the five-book Torah took shape during the Babylonian exile and the period that followed. We know that in the middle of the fifth century in Jerusalem, less than a century after Cyrus' decree, there was a public reading of "the book of the Torah of Moses," which was probably close to the Torah we know today. Its public reading served the same function that the public reading of Deuteronomy had served almost two centuries before, to establish the book being read as an authoritative text.

But while Deuteronomy enjoyed the patronage of a Davidic king, Ezra's Torah was backed by the Persians. For Ezra, described in the Bible as "a scribe skilled in the Torah of Moses" and a priest, was also a Persian civil servant, and he had come to Jerusalem as the emissary of the Persian crown. In other words, the emergence of the Torah as a central Jewish institution in the period after the exile took place at the initiative of the foreign ruler. Because the Persians granted considerable internal autonomy to their subject peoples, they needed clarity about the laws of those peoples. Thus they required civil servants such as Ezra, experts in the laws of a subject people, and they appear to have supported Ezra's attempt to elicit communal acknowledgment of the authority of the Torah. It appears that they were less enthusiastic about the trouble Ezra caused as a result of his effort to enforce a prohibition on marriage between men from the community of returnees and local women that he understood as the mandate of the Torah, though much of the community would have disagreed. Ezra's unexplained disappearance from the scene in the biblical account may suggest that his Persian bosses, who had sent him to stabilize the community, were not happy with the turmoil he caused with his attempt to send away wives he viewed as foreign along with their children. Nonetheless the Persians do not appear to have blamed the Torah itself, which remained the established law of the Jewish people throughout the Persian period and beyond.

From the time of Ezra, then, two institutions stood at the center of Judaism, the Temple and the Torah. The institutions were intertwined with each other. Much of the Torah is devoted to the laws of sacrifice and other rituals that take place in the Temple. Furthermore, as the figure of Ezra demonstrates, there was considerable overlap between the officials responsible for the two institutions; though priesthood was a hereditary status in ancient Israel, priests are prominent among the Torah experts of the Second Temple period whose names and ancestry are known to us.

But the two institutions also stood in a certain tension with each other, as the career of Nehemiah demonstrates. Nehemiah was a highly placed Jewish courtier who played on his friendship with the Persian king to arrange for his own appointment as governor of Yehud. He arrived in Jerusalem in this capacity shortly after Ezra's visit. Unlike Ezra, he was not a priest, but he was far more effective than Ezra in accomplishing his goals. He succeeded both in fortifying Jerusalem and in imposing a number of reforms of communal life. Upon returning to Jerusalem from a visit to the Persian capital, Nehemiah reports, he discovered that the high priest Eliashib had given Tobiah the Ammonite use of a room in the Temple. Though Tobiah was a friend of Eliashib, he was a long-standing enemy of Nehemiah, and Nehemiah did not hesitate to throw him out of the space Eliashib had given him. As the governor of Yehud, with the power of the state behind him, Nehemiah could do as he wished. Nonetheless in his memoir he chose to justify his actions by appealing to the Torah of Moses: "On that day they read from the book of Moses in the hearing of the people; and in it was found written that no Ammonite or Moabite should ever enter the assembly of God" (Neh. 13:1). The meaning of the passage to which Nehemiah alludes, Deuteronomy 23:3, is not crystal clear, but it appears to prohibit the offspring of marriages between Israelites and Ammonites from participating in the Israelite cult until the tenth generation. Nehemiah, however, reads the prohibition as demanding the exclusion of Ammonites and Moabites from the Temple building.

Eliashib's response to Nehemiah's attack has not come down to us, but he surely could have claimed that the Temple was his domain and that Nehemiah had no business meddling. As the high priest, he knew far better than Nehemiah, a layman, what was permitted in that domain and what was not, for he was heir to priestly tradition learned at the knee of his father and his grandfather. If it were not for the written text, Eliashib would surely have had the better of the argument, though Nehemiah with his governor's power could still have done as he wished. But the written text, read aloud for all to hear, allowed Nehemiah to trump Eliashib's claims based on the ancestral traditions of the priesthood in the name of preserving the holiness of the Temple. Thus, on the one hand the Torah provided a warrant for the Temple and its cult, but on the other hand it left the Temple and its officials vulnerable to criticism for failing to fulfill their duties. That criticism was especially likely to come from those learned in the Torah, though many scribes, like Ezra, were also priests by ancestry. We shall see that criticism of the priests and the way they run the Temple is an important theme of some apocalypses, but, as with Nehemiah's criticism, this later criticism of the cult grows out of the desire to see the highest standards maintained for priesthood and Temple.

Prophecy did not disappear with the destruction of the First Temple. Indeed, as we have seen, there were prophets who comforted the exiled Israelites in Babylonia while other prophets played an important role in encouraging the community of the return to complete the building of the new Temple. Nonetheless the authoritative status of the written text of the Torah made prophecy less important. Now that the Torah was publicly available, it did not take a prophet to discern God's will. Instead textual interpretation became increasingly central. It is significant that the prophecies of Zechariah from the time of the building of the Second Temple take the form not of the direct speech of the Lord typical of prophecy before the destruction but of visions to be deciphered by an angel. As we shall see, the apocalypses develop still further the idea of prophecy as interpretation.

In 333 Alexander of Macedon began the campaigns that made him ruler of lands from Greece to India by bringing an end to the Persian empire; by 332 Yehud was under his control. With Alexander's death in 323, his vast empire was divided among his generals. By the beginning of the third century BCE Judea, as it was now known, had fallen to the lot of Ptolemy, whose realm was centered in Egypt, and it remained under the rule of his descendants until 200 BCE, when Antiochus III, a descendant of Alexander's general Seleucus, wrested it from them. The arrival of Alexander and the Greeks brought some important changes to the Jews, including intensified contact with Greek culture. But the autonomy the Jews had enjoyed under the Persians remained largely in tact under Ptolemaic rule and the first decades of Seleucid rule. Josephus, the Jewish historian who wrote at the end of the first century CE, tells us that when Alexander passed through Jerusalem on his way to Egypt, he confirmed the right of the Jews to live by their "ancestral laws" (*Jewish Antiquities* 11.329–38). Other aspects of Josephus' account, such as Alexander's report that he recognized the high priest as the man who had appeared to him in a dream encouraging him as he began on his course of conquest, are likely Jewish wishful thinking, but there is no reason to doubt that Alexander planned to continue Persian policy toward the internal affairs of the Jews. The policy appears to have continued under Ptolemy I, who gained control of Judea around 300 BCE, though his successors, in keeping with their effort at centralization, may not have granted official recognition of Judean autonomy or of the political role of the high priests. Yet if observance of the laws of the Torah then became voluntary, there is no indication that the Torah suddenly lost its authority nor the high priests their prestige. When the Seleucid monarch Antiochus III conquered Judea in 200 BCE, he confirmed again the right of the Jews to live by their ancestral laws.

Chapter 2

The Book of the Watchers and Ascent to Heaven

The Book of the Watchers is not the earliest apocalypse – the Astronomical Book, also attributed to the patriarch Enoch, preceded it – but it is a good place to begin the discussion of apocalyptic literature. Although its combination of form and content is quite distinctive, it was extremely influential. All later apocalypses involving ascent to heaven are indebted to it either directly or indirectly, as are later apocalypses attributed to Enoch whether they involve ascent or not. Fragments of the original Aramaic of the work are preserved among the Dead Sea Scrolls, and much of the Book of the Watchers is extant in Greek translation, but for the complete work we must rely on the Ethiopic translation of the Greek, in which it appears as chapters 1–36 of an anthology of Enochic apocalypses known to scholars as 1 Enoch. As we have seen, the Book of the Watchers as a complete work dates from no later than the beginning of the second century BCE and perhaps somewhat earlier, but some of the sources on which it drew are considerably earlier, perhaps as early as the end of the Persian period. In other words, the Book of the Watchers took shape during the period of Ptolemaic rule in Judea, a period about which we know very little, and it reached its final form either shortly before or just after Judea fell to the Seleucids. It thus predates the transformative events of the Hellenistic reform and the Maccabean Revolt that shaped the book of Daniel, which are discussed in the next chapter.

The Descent of the Watchers

The point of departure for the Book of the Watchers is the story of the descent of the sons of God to take wives from among the daughters of man (1 Enoch 6–11), of which Genesis 6:1–4 offers a condensed version. The Book of the Watchers alludes to this enigmatic biblical passage, but it is hard to understand its account as derived solely from exegesis. Rather, the Book of the Watchers appears to be drawing on a larger set of traditions that surface only briefly in Genesis. The biblical narrative hints that the marriage of sons of God and the daughters of man had deleterious consequences for humanity by placing the story immediately before its account of the Flood. In the Book of the Watchers the devastating effects of this violation of the order of the universe by the sons of God, which it identifies as watchers, a class of angels known to us from the book of Daniel as well, are quite explicit. The devastation is caused most obviously by the offspring of the divine beings and their human wives, giants with insatiable appetites who devour not only beasts but humans as well. As human beings cry out in anguish, God sends his archangels to punish the watchers for their transgressions and to bring a flood to cleanse the earth of all the wrongdoing that has taken place upon it so that it will enjoy peace and fertility forever. Presumably this permanent state of blessedness is intended as description of the distant future, after the Last Judgment (1 Enoch 24:3, 26:3), not of the post-Flood state of the world.

Genesis' story of the descent of the sons of God stands apart from its context. The rest of the primeval history (Genesis 1–11) attempts to explain how the ordered and good world of creation (Genesis 1) became the world as we know it. But all of the other stories firmly place the blame for the sorry state of affairs on humanity: Adam and Eve's disobedience of God's commands, Cain's inability to tolerate God's apparent preference for Abel, and the sins of Noah's generation before the Flood; and Ham's violation of Noah's nakedness and the building of the Tower of Babel after the Flood. Alone among these stories Genesis 6:1–4 describes disobedience originating not on earth but in heaven. Indeed the compression of the narrative may reflect an effort to

nod at a well-known legend about the origins of evil in
without allowing it to disrupt the biblical account's e
human disobedience by giving it too much attention.
the Book of the Watchers, on the other hand, places t
the human predicament not in human disobedience or un...
ingness to accept the limits of being human but rather in divine
unwillingness to accept those boundaries. The descent of the
watchers emerges as an alternative to Adam and Eve's disobedience in the Garden of Eden as the source of evil in the world,
with divine beings rather than humans responsible for the introduction of forbidden knowledge. Thus the explanation for the
origins of evil in the Book of the Watchers stands in considerable
tension with the view that dominates the primeval history of
Genesis and the Hebrew Bible more generally.

Yet the Book of the Watchers can also be read as moderating
this understanding of the origins of evil. After the account of the
marriages of the watchers to women and the destruction wrought
by their fearsome offspring, there comes a list of watchers and the
skills or knowledge each one revealed to humanity. The negative
consequences of some of the skills, such as the arts of war, are evident, but others, such as metalworking and the manufacture of
cosmetics, are basic to civilization; some types of knowledge, such
as knowledge of the cutting of roots and interpreting the signs of
the heavens, are closely connected to magic and the supernatural
world. The list implies that knowledge that should not have been
revealed to human beings is to blame for what went wrong on
earth. The list apparently derives from a different source from the
account that blames the watchers' marriages and the giants who
result from them, though the Book of the Watchers has made
some effort to integrate the two explanations. The first angel
mentioned on the list, Asael, is said to have revealed the arts of
war, jewelry-making, and the making of cosmetics. In its only
comment on the angelic revelations, the Book of the Watchers
notes here that the sons of men began to make these items for
themselves and their daughters so that their daughters led the
holy ones astray (1 Enoch 8:1).

If the narrative of chapters 6–8 is read chronologically, the
revelation of forbidden knowledge follows on the watchers'

descent for purposes of marriage. But the Book of the Watchers' comment suggests another reading. In this reading chapter 8 becomes a sort of flashback that implies that with the revelation of techniques of beautification to humanity, women used those techniques to seduce the angels, thus bringing about the birth of the giants and the havoc that they caused. In this understanding of the origins of evil, the transgressions of the watchers came first, but human beings were quick to follow, with the behavior of women then contributing to the further transgressions of the watchers.

The power of the story is clear: it absolves humanity of the blame, or, in the reading that places the revelation of knowledge first, some of the blame, for the evils around us. By the end of the second century BCE the Book of Jubilees had added to the story an element that became extremely popular: the survival of the spirits of the giants after the death of their bodies as demons that lead humanity astray and cause human misfortune. The idea of demons as the result of the marriage of watchers and women proved extremely fruitful. The second-century CE Christian apologist Justin Martyr, for example, suggested that the gods worshiped by pagans were the fallen watchers and their demonic offspring.

Enoch and the Calendar

The Book of the Watchers introduces its hero at the very beginning (1 Enoch 1–5), where he offers a speech about the Last Judgment that contrasts the faithfulness of nature with the faithlessness of humanity. But Enoch is notably absent from the story of the descent of the watchers, a clear indication that this story developed independently of Enoch traditions. The connection is established by the authors of the next unit (1 Enoch 12–16); like the authors of the narrative of the descent of the watchers, they drew on traditions that stand behind a passage in Genesis as well as on the passage itself. The passage from Genesis relevant to this unit of the Book of the Watchers is the brief notice of the extraordinary career of the patriarch in Genesis 5:21–4. The other patriarchs who form the links in the genealogies of the primeval history live a certain number of years, beget their first son, live many years more, beget more sons and daughters, and die. Not so Enoch. After begetting Methuselah, Enoch "walked with God; and he was not, for God took him" (Gen. 5:24) at the youthful age – by antediluvian standards – of 365.

The number of years of Enoch's life on earth points to the calendar, and though Enoch's association with the calendar is only hinted at in the Book of the Watchers, it is central to the earlier Astronomical Book. The Astronomical Book consists of a detailed account of the movements of sun and moon, presented as a revelation to Enoch by the angel Uriel; the Aramaic fragments show that the Ethiopic is an abridgment of an even longer original. The work demonstrates how the movements of the moon can be coordinated with the 364-day year it attributes to the sun, but it makes no mention at all of such obvious Jewish calendrical concerns as the Sabbath or the festivals. It is matter-of-fact in tone even in its criticism of those who fail to add a day between each of its 90-day quarters, thus producing a year of only 360 days. The only passage in which the rhetoric becomes more heated is one that blames the sins of humanity for the failure of the heavenly bodies to appear on time (1 Enoch 80). This passage is widely regarded as a later addition, and it suggests that advocates of the Astronomical Book's calendar had come to realize that their 364-day year too was shorter than nature required.

Unfortunately we do not know what kind of calendar was in use in the Temple during the early Second Temple period so it is difficult to say what the Astronomical Book is responding to. The Torah's festival calendars appear to contain both solar and lunar elements: the celebration of the new month reflects concern for the moon, while festivals linked to the agricultural year require a solar calendar. But it is worth remembering that the Torah's most important calendrical innovations, the Sabbath and the seven-day week, are entirely man-made, with no connection at all to nature. The beauty of the 364-day year is that it consists of exactly fifty-two weeks so that the festivals of the biblical calendar fall out on the same day of the week year after year. This is not the case for the 365-day solar calendar, the lunar calendar, or the later rabbinic combination of the two, the one still in use among Jews for religious purposes. The disadvantage of the 364-day year, as the current form of the Astronomical Book admits, is that it does not correspond to reality, thus gradually pulling the festivals out of alignment with the seasons to which they belong.

After the Maccabean Revolt in the middle of the second century BCE, the Temple authorities seem to have made use of a combination solar-lunar calendar. The Book of Jubilees engages in a vigorous polemic against such a calendar in favor of a 364-day calendar, and the Dead Sea Scrolls also subscribe to a 364-day calendar. The dissonance between the 364-day calendar revealed to Enoch in the Astronomical Book and Enoch's 365-year life span according to the Torah is evident, but it is not clear whether this difference reflects a polemic against a 364-day calendar already associated with Enoch inserted in a late stage of the editing of the Torah or simply a variant tradition.

Enoch's Ascent and the Heavenly Temple

Enoch makes his appearance in the narrative of the Book of the Watchers when the watchers who remain in heaven commission him to deliver a message of condemnation to their fellow watchers who have descended to earth (1 Enoch 12). Although the watchers address Enoch by his professional title, scribe, the errand on which they send him requires him to speak, not to write. But scribal skills are required for the task the fallen watchers ask him to undertake upon hearing his message, the drawing up of a petition for mercy to be taken before the Lord. Enoch writes the petition, seats himself by the waters of Dan, and proceeds to recite the words of the petition until he falls asleep (1 Enoch 13). In his sleep he is taken up to heaven to stand before the divine throne (1 Enoch 14). As we have seen, the Torah notes that God took Enoch, presumably to heaven, and it also describes Elijah's ascent to heaven at the end of his earthly career. But the Book of the Watchers is the first ancient Jewish text to narrate an ascent in detail.

In the period of the First Temple, God was understood to be present and available to his people in the Jerusalem Temple. Thus, for example, the prophet Isaiah in the middle of the eighth century BCE describes receiving his commission during an encounter in the Temple, where the Lord sits enthroned, surrounded by the heavenly host. The loss of the Temple thus meant that God's presence was no longer constantly available in Jerusalem. The chariot-throne of Ezekiel's famous vision, composed of four-faced creatures with wheels in place of feet, provides the divine presence, now homeless, with a means of conveyance so that it can travel anywhere it wills, including to Babylonia by the River Chebar, where it appears to Ezekiel.

Although the Second Temple had been standing for centuries by the time the Book of the Watchers was composed, it never filled the gap left by the First Temple. The book of Ezra describes a mixed reaction to the Second Temple from the people assembled as the foundation stone was laid in 520 BCE: while some shouted with joy, those who remembered the First Temple wept (Ezra 3:10–13). Later in the Second Temple period, priests are often accused of polluting the Temple. Some texts go so far as to suggest that the Second Temple was polluted from the very start. Thus it is perhaps not surprising that the Book of the Watchers sends Enoch not to Jerusalem but to heaven to find God's presence.

Yet heaven as the Book of the Watchers describes it turns out to be a temple. Of course, anywhere God dwells is by definition a temple since "house of the Lord" is one of the terms by which the Bible refers to the Jerusalem Temple. But the ascent of the Book of the Watchers has in mind more than this tautology. When Enoch arrives in heaven he enters a marvelous building complex composed of fire and ice. But despite the awesome construction materials, which send Enoch into a state of fear and trembling, the structure of the complex – an outer wall and a house within a house – echoes the tripartite structure shared by the wilderness tabernacle of the Torah, the Jerusalem Temple of the book of Kings, and the vision of the restored temple of the book of Ezekiel. Enoch sees cherubim on the ceiling of the middle chamber of the heavenly building; cherubim decorate the walls of all three biblical sanctuaries. When Enoch finally reaches the entrance to the inner building, he falls prostrate in awe and fear at the sight he sees there, the Lord clothed in a brilliant white garment, seated

a throne of cherubim. It is remarkable sign of Ezekiel's influ-
e on the Book of the Watchers that the throne has wheels
despite the fact that is fixed in heaven.

Just as the earthly Temple has priests, so too does the heavenly
one. Enoch sees a multitude of angels before the divine throne,
but only "the holy ones of the watchers" are permitted to approach
it. Though these angels are not explicitly identified as priests,
"approach" is a technical term for priestly service in the Torah.
Further, when God responds to the petition of the fallen watchers, he begins by rebuking them for asking a human being to
intercede on their behalf when it was their duty to intercede for
humans (1 Enoch 15:2). Intercession, mediation between the
divine and the human realm, is a priestly task.

Though Enoch ascends to heaven in his professional capacity of
scribe to deliver the petition he has drawn up, God's words con-
firm another aspect of Enoch's identity, an aspect implied by his
safe progress through the heavenly temple. The Torah cautions
that only a priest is permitted to pass beyond the courtyard to the
central chamber of the Temple where sacrifices are performed:
"The stranger who approaches shall die" (Num. 18:7; my trans.).
Thus, though at the time in which the Book of the Watchers is set
there was as yet no temple on earth and therefore no priesthood,
Enoch must nonetheless be a priest as well as a scribe to permit
him access to the inside of the heavenly temple. Recall that Ezra
the scribe, who established the Torah at the center of Judaism,
was also a priest by ancestry. Indeed the combination of priestly
ancestry and scribal profession is not uncommon in the Second
Temple period.

We left Enoch prostrate before the divine throne, a position
from which an angel soon raises him. Now God orders Enoch to
tell the watchers that their petition has been rejected and con-
demns them for abandoning heaven for the sake of their wives.
In light of the priestly function of the watchers, some scholars
have suggested that this condemnation of the behavior of the
watchers is intended to criticize priests of the Jerusalem Temple
for marrying foreign women. But by the time the Book of the
Watchers took shape foreign women were understood as forbidden to all Jewish men, and such behavior by a significant portion

of the priesthood thus seems unlikely. I would suggest instead that the Book of the Watchers was criticizing a practice most Jews and most priests believed was perfectly acceptable, marriage to Jewish women who were not from priestly families. The view that priests should marry only women of priestly ancestry is clearly a minority view, but it is attested in other works found among the Dead Sea Scrolls. It appears to be based on a particularly strict reading of the laws of priestly marriage in Leviticus. The fact that some watchers remain in heaven as their fellows descend to earth to marry women suggests that the Book of the Watchers does not view all priests as guilty of wrongdoing.

Of course, the parallel between watchers and priests is not perfect. Marriage itself is wrong for the watchers, since, as God notes in his condemnation of the fallen watchers, marriage is unnecessary for immortal beings; human priests are restricted in their choice of wives but they are expected to marry. Furthermore, it should be emphasized that the depiction of Enoch as a priest is a strong indication of the high regard in which the Book of the Watchers holds the priesthood as an institution even if it criticizes actual priests for failing to live up to its standards.

Finally, it should be noted that the Book of the Watchers understands Enoch not only as scribe and priest. His vision of God enthroned and his role as God's messenger show clearly that he should be understood as a prophet as well. Thus according to the Book of the Watchers Enoch embodies the three central types of religious authority.

The Journey to the Ends of the Earth

From his place before the divine throne Enoch departs on a journey in which he travels to the ends of the earth and sees things inaccessible to other human beings (1 Enoch 17–36). The journey is actually a combination of two sources. The first (1 Enoch 17–19) is brief and often opaque. The second (1 Enoch 20–36) reworks the first, recounting the sights more clearly and at greater length, and adds new sights. The journey to the ends of the earth seems to have taken shape independently of the ascent to heaven and is linked to it only loosely. One of the last sights Enoch sees in the first journey is the place of punishment of the watchers, the place to which he would have to travel to deliver God's response to their petition (1 Enoch 19), and a very similar version of the watchers' punishment appears again at the beginning of the second account of the journey (1 Enoch 21). Yet in neither instance does Enoch fulfill the task with which God entrusted him by informing the watchers of the rejection of their petition.

Enoch travels to the ends of the earth in the company of the archangels, who serve as his guides, explaining the sights he sees: "This is...," "These are...," "This place is...." These demonstrative explanations, usually in response to Enoch's questions, reflect ancient modes of dream and vision interpretation known from the Hebrew Bible and elsewhere in the ancient Near East. In making use of them the Book of the Watchers suggests that the sights Enoch sees are also divine revelations.

As just noted, both sources of the journey to the ends of the earth include a stop at the place where the watchers endure their punishment. In the second source, the reward and punishment of human beings also figures as a central concern, and, shortly after he sees the punishment of the watchers, Enoch is taken to see the chambers in which the souls of the dead are stored as they await the Last Judgment (1 Enoch 22). The chamber in which the souls of the righteous are kept has light and a fountain; the other chambers are dark.

Soon Enoch comes to a high mountain with a beautiful tree nearby and six mountains around it (1 Enoch 24). At the eschaton God will descend to that mountain to judge humanity. The tree, Enoch is told, will then be transplanted to the Temple where the righteous will enjoy its fruit. Next Enoch turns to the "center of the earth," that is, Jerusalem, where he sees a beautiful mountain covered with trees and a deep and barren valley (1 Enoch 25–6). The "cursed valley" is Gehinnom, the valley in Jerusalem in which, according to the prophet Jeremiah, Israelites sacrificed their children to the pagan god Molech. There, after the Last Judgment, the wicked will suffer their punishment as the righteous look on. The beautiful mountain, presumably the future dwelling place of the righteous, must be Mount Zion, the Temple mount.

These sights are the first clear expression of a belief in
mortem reward and punishment in Jewish literature. They
a significant departure from the biblical picture of the ?
descending to Sheol, where the righteous and the wicked a
endure a sort of shadow existence. The sights reflect an understanding of the fate of souls after death as having two stages: stor-
age in the appropriate chamber to await the Last Judgment,
which already constitutes reward or punishment, and then a
more intense reward or punishment after the Last Judgment. The
impetus for the new picture can be found in earlier biblical discussion of the fate of the righteous, and the emphasis on the
immortality of the soul in some strands of Greek thought may
also have had an impact.

The other central theme of the second source of the journey is
the wonders of nature. After leaving Jerusalem, Enoch travels
into the desert to the east, which is full of wonderful spice trees
(1 Enoch 27–31). Finally he comes to the "paradise of righteousness," where he sees a large and magnificent tree (1 Enoch 32).
This, the angel explains,

> is the tree of wisdom from which your father of old and your
> mother of old, who were before you, ate and learned wisdom. And
> their eyes were opened, and they knew that they were naked, and
> they were driven from the garden. (1 Enoch 32:6)

Presumably the author of this portion of the journey felt it impossible to avoid mention of one of the most important locations in
Jewish mythic geography, the Garden of Eden, and with it, the
story of Adam and Eve's disobedience, but he has done everything
he can to minimize its impact. He has already moved the tree of
life to a new location, for surely the tree that will provide fruit to
the righteous at the eschaton is nothing other than the tree of life.
Here, the version of the story of the expulsion from Eden that the
angel offers Enoch in explanation of the tree of knowledge avoids
mentioning that eating from this tree was an act of disobedience.
Thus the Book of the Watchers manages to incorporate the dominant biblical story of the origins of evil into its narrative while
keeping it subordinate to the story of the watchers.

Enoch continues on his journey, traveling north, west, south, and finally east yet again. As he travels he sees great beasts and birds and also the earthly gates of meteorological and cosmological phenomena: the gates of the stars and the gates of winds and hail, rain, and snow (1 Enoch 33–6). Upon seeing these wonders, Enoch praises God for creating them. There is no mention of the gates of the sun and moon so central to the calendrical revelation of the Astronomical Book, and if we had to rely on the Book of the Watchers alone we would have only a few hints at the association of Enoch with the calendar.

The idea of the natural world as testifying to the greatness of its creator became particularly important to the Israelites during the Babylonian exile. To those who saw recent events as calling into question God's strength and power, the prophet of Second Isaiah asks, "Lift up your eyes on high and see: who created these?" (Isa. 40:26). He is confident of the answer, the same answer offered by one of the psalms: "The heavens declare the glory of God, and the firmament proclaims the work of his hands" (Ps. 19:1; my trans.). This idea is prominent in biblical Wisdom works, particularly some of the psalms and the book of Proverbs. But there was a more skeptical side to biblical wisdom as well. The book of Job, written in the wake of the exile, suggests that God's plans are beyond human understanding, and God uses the wonders of nature to silence Job: "Where were you when I laid the foundation of the earth? ... Have you entered the storehouses of the snow or have you seen the storehouses of the hail ...?" (Job 38:4, 22). Here the wonders of creation are represented as hidden from human beings just as wisdom is hidden, and God the creator is under no obligation to explain himself to a mere human being.

The Book of the Watchers is neither as optimistic as the Psalmist about the clarity with which nature speaks of its creator nor as pessimistic as the book of Job. On the one hand, the sights that Enoch sees are not available to all humanity: "I, Enoch, alone saw the visions, the extremities of all things. And no one among humans has seen as I saw," Enoch says at the end of the first journey (1 Enoch 19:3). On the other hand, God permits the revelation of the wonders of nature to one human being, and through his account the rest of humanity can join in "bless[ing] the Lord of glory, who has wrought great and glorious wonders" (1 Er 36:4). In contrast to the knowledge revealed to humanity by watchers, the wonders revealed to Enoch by the angels lead to sin and disaster but to the recognition of God's greatness.

Enoch Between Humanity and the Angels

Angels appear in biblical literature from the period of the First Temple as messengers of God and as members of his heavenly entourage. In the period after the exile angels multiply and become a more central part of the Jewish picture of the world. Before the exile the visions of the prophets Amos and Jeremiah are interpreted by God himself; after the exile an angel interprets the visions of the prophet Zechariah. Before the exile, angels remain anonymous, even such outstanding angels as the commander of the Lord's army whom Joshua encounters outside Jericho. After the exile Satan appears in the books of Zechariah and Job; at this early stage of his development he is merely the accuser, as his name indicates, the prosecuting attorney in the heavenly courtroom rather than an enemy of God and humanity. Not long after, the leading angels are given names – Michael, Gabriel, Raphael, Uriel, and so on – names found in the Astronomical Book, the Book of the Watchers, Tobit, and other works from before the Maccabean Revolt. Sometime after the revolt the Book of Jubilees offers a list of the various types of angels created on the first day. If God was no longer available in the Jerusalem Temple but only in its heavenly counterpart, the proliferation of angels meant that they at least were nearby.

But the picture of the universe in the Book of the Watchers is more complicated than the one I have just sketched. One striking aspect is the permeability of the borders between humanity and the divine sphere. The narrative is set in motion when the watchers cross the boundary by descending to earth with disastrous consequences for themselves and for humanity. On the other hand, in his ascent to heaven and journey to the ends of the earth in the company of the archangels, Enoch crosses the boundary to positive effect. Although these trips lack concrete results other than the rejection of the petition of the fallen watchers, they reassure readers that God still sits enthroned in heaven, that the heavenly temple continues to function, and that the created world testifies to God's greatness. Perhaps most important, the account of Enoch's ability to mediate between angels and God, to stand before the divine throne, and to be a travel companion to angels tells readers that humanity, or at least one of its outstanding representatives, is the equal of the angels. Though his ability to cross the boundary between the human and the divine spheres does not imply that ordinary human beings can do so, it does serve as an indication of the heights to which human beings can rise. In the end, the Book of the Watchers suggests that angels do not necessarily belong above humanity in the hierarchy of being and that human contact with God need not be mediated by angels.

The Milieu of the Book of the Watchers

The Dead Sea Scrolls were the library of a small community at a place called Qumran. The Qumran community regarded its members as children of light while it saw all others, Jews and gentiles alike, as children of darkness. It is thus a classic instance of a sect in the sociological sense: a group that claims to have exclusive access to the truth and views everyone outside the sect as lost. Some scholars have taken the fact that the Book of the Watchers was copied by the Qumran community as an indication that it is sectarian in outlook. I believe that they are mistaken. Even as the Book of the Watchers criticizes the behavior of some priests, its description of the heavenly temple, in which some of the watchers remain at their stations, shows that it does not condemn all priests. Furthermore, though the ascent rests on the premise that God is most fully available in heaven, there is nothing in the work to suggest that the Jerusalem Temple itself was defiled by the presence of the priests it criticizes. In the view of the Qumran community, in contrast, the Jerusalem Temple was so polluted that the community would not make use of it. Nor is the eschatology of the Book of the Watchers sectarian in tone. Those who will survive the cleansing of the earth are "the righteous," not "the elect" or "the wise" or a term with a narrower focus, and eventually the original righteous, presumably Jews, will be joined by all nations (1 Enoch 10:21).

Many scholars claim that the Enoch literature, including the Book of the Watchers, stands apart from the Torah, offering revealed wisdom rather than the laws of the Torah as a guide for life. I find this claim difficult to accept. I limit my comments here to the Book of the Watchers. Because of the period in which it is set, the Book of the Watchers cannot make explicit reference to the Torah without engaging in anachronism. But the claim that the Torah is not central to its worldview is simply untenable. As we have seen, the Book of the Watchers makes use of traditions that stand behind the text of the Torah, but it also engages the text of the Torah for its picture of the angels' descent and Enoch's ascent. The priestly etiquette of the heavenly temple is deeply informed by the priestly source of the Torah, and the depiction of the heavenly temple draws on the Torah as well as other biblical sources. If I am correct, the Book of the Watchers' criticism of priestly marriage practices is based on exegesis of a law of the Torah. Furthermore, at the very point at which tension between the Book of the Watchers and the Torah is clearest, the theory of the origins of evil, the editors of the Book of the Watchers work hard to reduce the tension by allowing for the integration of human sinfulness into a narrative that emphasizes angelic transgression.

Some scholars have suggested that the authors of the Book of the Watchers were priests because of their admiration for the institution of the Temple, the earthly replica of God's heavenly abode, and for the role of priest, and their criticism of priests who behave improperly. But the importance of the Temple was recognized by virtually all ancient Jews, and just as Nehemiah, a layman, attempted to hold the high priest to the highest standards, so any pious Jew would demand that priests follow the rules laid down for them in the Torah. Thus the authors of the Book of the Watchers need not have been priests. There is one aspect of their hero's identity that the book's authors clearly did share, however: like Enoch, they were scribes. Indeed, the scribal skills they demonstrate go well beyond Enoch's knowledge of how to draw up a petition, for they composed their consideration of the origins of evil and the place of human beings in the universe by drawing on a variety of preexisting sources and traditions, making extensive use of Scripture and interpreting its narratives and laws.

Consideration of the authors of the Book of the Watchers also confronts us with the problem of pseudepigraphy: why did people choose to write in the name of an ancient hero rather than in their own names? Some scholars have suggested that the authors of the apocalypses should be understood as prophets operating in an era in which prophecy was widely viewed as a thing of the past. Thus the apocalypses reflect actual prophetic experience including trances and ascents that are attributed to ancient heroes to improve the chances that they would receive a sympathetic hearing. The internal evidence of the Book of the Watchers and of the other apocalypses seems to me to point away from such an understanding. The range of sources on which the authors drew and the care with which they arranged them suggests that they were not recording their own experiences but rather, despite their use of an ancient hero, were operating as authors usually do.

The Book of the Watchers was extraordinarily influential. The story of the descent of the watchers goes on to play a significant role in a wide range of literature in antiquity. So too ascent becomes a central mode of receiving revelation in Jewish and Christian literature into the Middle Ages, and while the form of the journey to the ends of the earth has few imitators, its interests, especially the fate of souls after death, are an important theme in many later apocalypses. It is noteworthy, however, that the Book of the Watchers has rather little to say about the course of history and the end of the world. It clearly anticipates a final judgment, to which it alludes at a number of points, but it does little to provide its readers with a timetable of events that would allow them to locate themselves in relation to the eschaton. For that, we turn to the book of Daniel, the fountainhead of the other stream of apocalyptic tradition.

Chapter 3

The Book of Daniel and the Kingdom of the Holy Ones

The book of Daniel is the only apocalypse in the Hebrew Bible. Its inclusion is particularly noteworthy because it is the latest composition to become part of the Hebrew canon, and its presence calls attention to the exclusion of the earlier Book of the Watchers. Like the Book of the Watchers, Daniel is a composite work, but unlike the Book of the Watchers, the work as a whole can be dated with some precision to the time of the Maccabean Revolt (167–163 BCE), which is described up to its midpoint in considerable detail, though in veiled terms, in the visions that form the second half of the book.

Like the Book of the Watchers, Daniel takes as its hero a famous figure of the past, a wise and righteous man about whom many stories were already in circulation. There are some signs that Daniel was not originally a Jewish figure: Ezekiel mentions Dan'el, a slightly different spelling of the name, together with Noah and Job, one pre-Israelite, the other non-Israelite, as three particularly righteous men, and some scholars have suggested that Daniel is connected to a figure with the same name in an ancient Ugaritic epic. But whatever his origins, by the middle of the second century BCE Daniel had long been naturalized as a Jew. The stories about him place him in the Babylonian and Persian royal courts, where he serves as a wise man, a profession with some similarities to Enoch's profession of scribe. His task, and that of the other wise men with whom he serves, is not to provide the king with practical advice, but rather to interpret dreams and portents for him. While Daniel does not write, he does engage in interpretation.

As the career of Nehemiah demonstrates, Jewish courtiers were a historical reality in the Persian era. Like the book of Esther, the first part of the book of Daniel takes this reality as the point of departure for its stories about the encounter between Jews and pagan kings, Babylonian and Persian, and their courtiers. These stories about Daniel and his friends, fellow exiles from Judah, probably date from the late Persian or early Hellenistic period. In them Daniel repeatedly demonstrates the greatness of the God of Israel to the king and his court by interpreting dreams and signs after the other wise men have been unable to do so. Both Daniel and his friends demonstrate God's greatness in another way as well, by refusing to worship other gods even when threatened with death. Each chapter of Daniel 2–6 consists of a self-contained story about Daniel or his friends. All of these stories are in Aramaic, as is the first of Daniel's visions in chapter 7. The first chapter of the book, an introduction to the Daniel stories, and the three remaining visions (Daniel 8–12) are in Hebrew. The linguistic situation appears to reflect the desire of the author of the visions to provide a strong connection between the visions and the older stories to which he attached them. Thus he wrote an introduction to the stories and the book as a whole in Hebrew so that the book begins and ends in Hebrew, and he wrote the first vision in Aramaic to create a stronger link between the Aramaic tales and the Hebrew visions.

It is clear that there were more stories about Daniel in circulation in antiquity than made it into the biblical book. The Greek version of Daniel includes stories absent from the Hebrew/Aramaic book, and a previously unknown story about Daniel was found among the Dead Sea Scrolls. It appears, then, that the author of the book of Daniel chose some stories and rejected others for inclusion in his work, presumably on the basis of their relevance to his concerns. Thus, for example, the first of Daniel's visions (Daniel 7) takes up the four-kingdom schema of the dream of Nebuchadnezzar, the great Babylonian king, that provides the plot of the first of the court tales (Daniel 2). More generally, the role of Daniel's angelic interlocutor in interpreting his visions in the second part of the book echoes Daniel's own role as preter of the dreams of Nebuchadnezzar and the writing o wall in the stories.

But there are also significant differences between the ouʌoоĸ of the stories and the outlook of the visions. The heroes' encounters with death in the stories of the first half of the book have happy endings: angelic intervention saves Daniel's friends from the fiery furnace as it saves Daniel himself from the lions' den. In contrast, the final vision of the book of Daniel alludes to the martyrs of the Maccabean Revolt: "And those among the people who are wise shall make many understand, though they shall fall by the sword and flame, by captivity and plunder, for some days" (Dan. 11:33). Another notable feature of the stories, which they share with the book of Esther, is their relatively positive picture of the kings, who are sometimes foolish but rarely evil, in contrast to their manipulative courtiers, who instigate persecution of the Jews because of their jealousy. The visions, on the other hand, place great emphasis on the evil of the eschatological villain Antiochus IV.

The visions of the book of Daniel were written at an important turning point in Jewish history. As we have seen, the Persians allowed the Jews considerable internal autonomy. While the Ptolemies took a more centralized approach to government, the century of Ptolemaic rule did not cause major changes in the status of Torah or Temple. With the Seleucid conquest in 200 BCE, Antiochus III officially confirmed the right of the Jews to live by their ancestral laws. Yet within a few decades Antiochus IV issued a decree prohibiting the practice of Judaism. Polytheists were generally tolerant of the worship of other gods, and the decree was a rare instance of religious persecution in Greco-Roman antiquity. In the late third and early second centuries BCE the Romans clamped down on the worship of foreign deities and religious behavior that they saw as masking political conspiracy. But the Jews, especially in their own land, were the beneficiaries of the Greek and later Roman respect for antiquity that granted even their peculiar laws a certain status because of their undoubted age. Thus scholars have struggled to understand Antiochus' prohibition of Judaism. Antiochus called himself Antiochus Epiphanes,

"God made manifest"; his peculiar behavior led some of his contemporaries to refer to him instead as Antiochus Epimanes, "mad man." Yet his odd personality is surely not enough to account for the persecution of Judaism.

The persecution followed on events set in motion when Antiochus gave permission to a group of Jews led by Jason, the brother of the reigning high priest Onias III, to establish a *polis*, a Greek city, in Jerusalem. Jason also succeeded in having himself named high priest in his brother's place, though not long after he was replaced by Menelaus, another ambitious member of the *polis* party who lacked any tie to the high-priestly family but who offered an even larger bribe than Jason. The effort of these wealthy Jews to establish a *polis* reflects their desire to break down some of the boundaries between Jews and gentiles and to participate more fully in the life of the empire in which they lived. In granting their request Antiochus may have been motivated by genuine enthusiasm for Greek culture and the desire to spread it, but the bribes were surely a significant consideration as well. The new city, named in honor of Antiochus, was not physically distinct from the old Jerusalem, but it was a new legal entity, bound not by the ancestral laws of the Jews but by its own laws. Its founders immediately set up two of the central institutions of any Greek city, a gymnasium, where citizens met and exercised, and an ephebate, an official listing of young male citizens. With the establishment of the *polis* the members of the Jerusalem elite who were its citizens came to be governed by its laws rather than by the Torah. Yet for most Jews the ancestral laws remained the law of the land.

One theory about the persecution is that it came at the initiative of some of the advocates of *polis* and its way of life, who had become impatient with the reluctance of other Jews to embrace their agenda and enlisted royal power in the effort to bring backward Jews into conformity with their views. In this theory the Maccabean Revolt was a response to the persecution. But it has also been suggested that the persecution was a response to a rebellion that was already under way. This reading of the sources finds hints that traditionalist Jews took up arms as fighting broke out between partisans of Menelaus and partisans of Jason. Since the rebels wished to make the ancestral laws once again binding on all Jews, Antiochus responded by forbidding all Jews to follow those laws.

The Four Kingdoms

Whatever the reasons for the persecution, there can be no doubt of its impact. Yet though the visions of the second half of the book of Daniel were written in response to the persecution, as far as they are concerned the actions most important for the course of human history take place in heaven. This message is repeated in each of the four units of the apocalyptic portion of the book. In his first vision (Daniel 7) Daniel sees four hideous beasts arise from the sea; these beasts represent the four kingdoms first encountered in Nebuchadnezzar's dream. The idea of a succession of four world kingdoms to be followed by a final kingdom in which righteousness triumphs probably originated in Persia after the Macedonian conquest. The kingdoms are not explicitly identified in this vision or in Nebuchadnezzar's dream, though there the first kingdom is identified as his. But it is clear from this passage and other information in the book of Daniel that the author, who believed that the Babylonian empire fell to Darius the Mede, understood the kingdoms as Babylonia, Media, Persia, and the Hellenistic empires.

The beasts Daniel sees coming out of the sea are no ordinary animals but are composed of aspects of the most terrifying of natural creatures: a lion with eagle's wings, a misshapen bear, a four-headed winged leopard. The description of the fourth beast with its ten horns alludes to specific rulers, culminating in the worst of them, the arrogant little horn that represents Antiochus IV. The rule of the horn comes to an end when God sits in judgment and gives dominion to a figure of human appearance. As we shall see in the next chapter, Daniel's presentation of the four-kingdoms schema with its association of the beasts with the sea and its particularly terrifying fourth beast proved to be extremely influential, leaving a mark on three apocalypses of the late first century CE, 4 Ezra, 2 Baruch, and the book of Revelation.

idea that the course of history was determined long ago is
al theme of the book of Daniel and of other apocalypses as
.. ᴅaniel 7 is set during the reign of Belshazzar, the last king of
Babylonia, when three of the four world empires are still in the
future. Of course for the author of Daniel and his contemporaries
the second and third empires were in the past, and the fourth had
run much of its course. The accuracy of the details the author was
thus able to insert into Daniel's visions of what still lay ahead
from the point of view of the narrative encouraged readers'
respect for the portion of the visions that predicted events that lay
in the future even from the author's point of view. So too in the
roughly contemporary Book of Dreams (1 Enoch 83–90) Enoch
has a vision of history from its beginning until the author's own
time in the middle of the second century BCE. The accurate
account of biblical history still in the future from Enoch's point of
view serves to inspire trust in his vision of the end. The same
technique appears in many apocalypses that concern themselves
with history such as the Apocalypse of Weeks in the Epistle of
Enoch, discussed later in this chapter, and 4 Ezra, discussed in the
next chapter.

The use of animal imagery in Daniel's vision of the four kingdoms is also part of a wider phenomenon, although elsewhere the
animals are more ordinary and true to life than those of Daniel 7.
The second vision of Daniel (Daniel 8) depicts the conflict of the
Greeks and the Persians as a battle between a he-goat and a great
ram; the only features of these animals that do not correspond to
nature are strange horns that reflect the history of the two kingdoms. The vision of history in the Book of Dreams represents individual human beings as animals. The type of animal and its color
indicate the character of the human being it represents. Before the
Flood, all human beings are represented as cattle, but the descendants of Seth are white cattle while the descendants of Cain are
black. The angels who descend to earth take the form of bulls, that
is, male human beings, so as to be able to mate with cows, female
human beings. The offspring of these bulls, the giants of the Book
of the Watchers, are not cattle but camels, elephants, and asses.
After the Flood, humanity divides into the ancestors of Israel and
the gentiles. Noah is a white bull who becomes a man; his three

sons are a white, a red, and a black bull. The red and black bulls beget lions, leopards, wolves, pigs, vultures, and many other types of wild animals. Ishmael is a wild ass, and Esau is a black wild boar. The descendants of Shem remain white bulls until the birth of Jacob, who is a white ram; all of his offspring and their descendants, the people of Israel, are sheep. At the end of days, all the animals are transformed into white cattle.

One Like a Son of Man

After the appearance of the fourth beast, Daniel sees God, described as "one ... ancient of days" (Dan. 7:9), take his seat in the heavenly court with books open before him. The picture of heaven as a royal palace is closely related to the picture of heaven as temple in the Book of the Watchers; both derive from an understanding of heaven as God's home. Daniel's picture of God and his entourage also shares significant details with the picture in the Book of the Watchers. In both works the throne and the one seated on it produce an impression of overwhelming brightness. Both works note the wheels on the throne, which go back to Ezekiel's vision of the chariot-throne, and the streams of fire issuing from beneath it. Both describe the whiteness of the garment God wears, though Daniel also notes the whiteness of God's beard. Perhaps most striking, the description of the multitude of angels serving God in the two works includes language that is virtually identical as far as preservation in different languages allows us to tell: "ten thousand times ten thousand stood before him" (1 Enoch 14:22; Dan. 7:10). Since there is nothing elsewhere in the book of Daniel to suggest that it made use of the Book of the Watchers, the best explanation of the similarities between the two works is shared traditions.

Following the decree of the court, the fourth beast is destroyed and eternal dominion is given to "one like a son of man" (Dan. 7:13), who arrives on the clouds of heaven; the phrase serves to contrast the human appearance of this being to the appearance of the four beasts from the sea. "Son of man" is a literal translation of a phrase that is an idiom for human being in both Hebrew and

Aramaic. The phrase is best known from the book of Ezekiel, where it is God's favored form of address to the prophet. In that context the term should probably be translated "mortal," that is, a human being in contrast to God. In Daniel, however, where the phrase is applied to a figure that travels on the clouds and that receives eternal dominion, the emphasis is clearly not on mortality in contrast to divinity but rather on human form in contrast to animal form.

The angelic interpreter of Daniel 7 identifies the final kingdom, represented by the figure of human appearance, as belonging to "the holy ones of the Most High" (Dan. 7:22; my trans.) The term "holy ones" could be understood to refer to the people of Israel, but it is more often used for angels in the literature of the Second Temple period. Thus the name of the final kingdom should probably be understood to mean the kingdom of the angels. Still, it is important to note that the angelic interpreter also speaks of the kingdom being given to "the people of the holy ones of the Most High" (Dan. 7:27; my trans.), that is, the people of Israel. This phrase expresses the understanding that the righteous on earth stand in close relationship to the angels in heaven, an understanding reflected in the depiction of Daniel's dealings with the angels and widespread in literature of the Second Temple period.

The beasts from the sea clearly represent kingdoms rather than individual kings, as the words of the angel about the fourth beast make clear (Dan. 7:23–4, despite Dan. 7:17, "four kings"). But unlike the beasts, whose strange appearance is engineered to symbolize dynasties and individual rulers, the figure of human appearance could represent either an individual or a kingdom. Some scholars have suggested that the figure is the angel Michael, who is elsewhere in the book of Daniel designated the guardian angel of the people of Israel (Dan. 12:1). Michael's relationship to Israel allows him to be understood as at once ruler and symbol of the eschatological kingdom.

The Four Kingdoms and Ancient Near Eastern Myth

Several of the elements of the vision of Daniel 7 derive from the world of ancient Near Eastern myth, which had a significant impact on the Hebrew Bible despite the biblical rejection of the polytheistic pantheons of the myths. One central ancient Near Eastern myth involves the defeat of the watery forces of chaos by a warrior god. In Canaanite myth, Ba'al, the god of thunder and fertility, defeats Yamm, the god of the sea, to secure his place among the gods, while in the ancient Babylonian myth, Marduk, the chief god of Babylon, defeats the chaos monster Tiamat in the course of creating the world. From the Torah to the prophets to Psalms, the association of the forces of chaos or evil with the sea and the divine warrior's subjugation of the watery forces inform not only the biblical understanding of creation but also of the exodus.

Elsewhere the Bible depicts God using imagery associated with the other great Canaanite god El, the father of the gods who presides over the Canaanite pantheon. Daniel 7's picture of God as an elderly figure seated on his throne among his heavenly courtiers recalls El's hoary beard and his epithet "judge." The figure of human appearance, on the other hand, is depicted engaged in the activity expressed in one of Ba'al's epithets, "rider on the clouds." In the Hebrew Bible one of the psalms refers to God himself as the rider on the clouds (Ps. 68:4), but the figure on the clouds in Daniel 7 is clearly subordinate to the elderly God. The relationship between God and the one like a son of man is something like the relationship between El, the father of the gods, and Ba'al, a younger member of his court, in the Canaanite pantheon. It is difficult to explain how knowledge of this relationship or the association of Ba'al with riding on the clouds reached the author of Daniel. The evidence for the transmission of the Canaanite myths during the first millennium BCE consists of some faint and somewhat distorted echoes, and although the myths have left an imprint on biblical texts, no one could deduce them from those texts. But the parallels are so compelling that it seems only reasonable to conclude that they were somehow available to the author of Daniel.

But even as Daniel's vision uses the imagery of polytheistic myth, it adapts it to its monotheistic worldview. It has room for only one god. While one of Ba'al's great achievements in Canaanite myth is his defeat in battle of the sea god Yamm, the one like a son of man does not defeat the fourth beast. Rather, the beast is destroyed by the sentence imposed by the Ancient of Days. The one like a son of man simply shows up to receive dominion from the Ancient of Days. The identification of the one like a son of man as Michael makes his passivity particularly striking because later in the book of Daniel Gabriel reports that Michael is engaged in battle with the angel representing Persia. But the vision of Daniel 7 leaves the eschatological drama entirely in the hands of God, who, despite his white hair, is quite capable of destroying his enemies.

We shall see in the next chapter that the one like a son of man captured the imagination of later apocalyptic writers, who gave him a more expansive role than he has in Daniel 7. But it is by no means unusual in apocalyptic literature for God to have a dominant role in the eschatological drama. In the Book of Dreams, the messiah appears only at the denouement of the drama, after God has already judged the righteous and the sinners and established the new temple on earth, while the Apocalypse of Weeks describes the end of history without any messianic figure at all.

Seventy Weeks of Years

Shortly after the Babylonian conquest of Jerusalem in 586 BCE, the prophet Jeremiah prophesied that the punishment of the Judeans would come to an end in seventy years. The prophecy appeared to be correct: as we have seen, Cyrus of Persia overthrew the Babylonian empire in 539 BCE, permitting the exiled Judeans to return to their land and rebuild their Temple, a task they finally completed in 515, almost exactly seventy years after the destruction of the First Temple. But for the author of the book of Daniel and his readers in the second century BCE, the limitations of that restoration were all too evident: while the Temple had been rebuilt, the people of Israel had never again enjoyed independence, and they themselves were now enduring a persecution unprecedented in their history. To address this problem the author of Daniel makes his hero the recipient of an angelic interpretation that reveals the correct understanding of the prophecy. In response to Daniel's distressed prayers, the angel Gabriel arrives with an explanation of the prophecy that shows that it has not failed, as Daniel's readers might have feared. For, Gabriel explains, the seventy years of the prophecy are not actual years but rather *weeks* of years. The concept of a week of years, although not the terminology, is familiar from the Torah, which decrees a year of rest for the Holy Land every seven years (Exod. 23:10–11; Lev. 25:1–7).

Gabriel's interpretation of Jeremiah's prophecy is hardly good news for the character Daniel, for whom even the seventieth year, much more the 490th, still lies in the future. But it would have cheered readers in the second century BCE enduring the persecution of Antiochus IV, although Gabriel's interpretation does present some chronological difficulties: 490 years from 586 BCE brings us to the very beginning of the first century BCE, several decades after the time our author was writing. Yet the interpretation of Jeremiah's prophecy makes it clear that our author expects history to have run its course in the space of three and a half years, a figure given considerable emphasis by its appearance elsewhere in the book as well (Dan. 7:25, 12:7). Presumably the discrepancy between a date 490 years after the Babylonian conquest and a date three and a half years from the moment the author is writing reflects the author's inexact knowledge of the chronology of the Persian and Hellenistic periods, not altogether surprising in the work of a man who attributed the fall of the Babylonian empire to Darius the Mede, and not without parallel in contemporary literature.

Eschatological Timetables in Other Second Temple Era Works

Eschatological timetables that order past and future in units of seven and its multiples play an important role in other apocalypses and works of the Second Temple period as far back as the Book of the Watchers, where God commands Michael to imprison the watchers for seventy generations, until the Last Judgment. Later Enochic works offer more highly developed eschatological timetables. The Book of Dreams divides the crucial era from shortly before the exile to the eschaton into seventy units presided over by seventy "shepherds," malevolent angels to whom God entrusts Israel's fate for that unhappy period. The first period consists of the rule of twelve shepherds. The vision does not provide enough detail to make it certain exactly when their reign begins, but it continues to the end of the Babylonian exile. Twenty-three shepherds rule from the time of the return from Babylonia to the coming of Alexander, and twenty-three more from Alexander to the beginning of the second century or the Maccabean Revolt; again the account is not entirely clear. The period leading up to the Last Judgment accounts for twelve more shepherds. It is difficult to coordinate this carefully balanced division of the seventy with what we know about the history of the era. It is possible that the shepherds were understood to rule for different lengths of time. It is also possible that the author's understanding of the Persian and Hellenistic eras, like that of the author of Daniel, was somewhat confused, and that a better knowledge of the period in question would not have permitted him to assign equal periods to each shepherd.

The Apocalypse of Weeks, a brief apocalypse presented as a revelation to Enoch, is an ambitious attempt to encompass all of history from beginning to end in "weeks" (1 Enoch 91, 93). The apocalypse was once an independent work, probably written shortly before the Maccabean Revolt, but it comes down to us as the beginning of the Epistle of Enoch (1 Enoch 92–105), which was composed some time after the Maccabean Revolt, probably before the turn of the era. Each week of the Apocalypse of Weeks is marked by a single event. Thus, for example, Enoch is born in the first week, the Flood comes in the second week, and Abraham lives in the third week. The seventh week, which is clearly the week during which the work was written, is described as a time of trouble, but at the end of this week the defeat of evil will begin. The eschatological battle between the righteous and the wicked will continue into the eighth week, and goodness will reign through the ninth and tenth weeks until a new heaven appears and the righteous enjoy weeks without number. Scholars have struggled to deduce the length of time of each week on the basis of the few pieces of information the Apocalypse of Weeks provides in combination with the biblical narratives to which it makes reference. One ingenious theory suggests that a week consists of 490 years, ten times the jubilee as it was understood in the Second Temple period.

Like the week of years, the jubilee, the cycle of seven times seven years ordained by the Torah (Lev. 25:8–17), had a major impact on the ordering of history in texts of the Second Temple period. In the Torah the cycle concludes in the fiftieth year with the jubilee, which brings "liberty" to all the inhabitants of the land: land returns to its original owners and slaves go free. Some scholars believe that the Torah understands the fiftieth year as the first year of the following jubilee cycle so that the jubilee cycle and seven-year sabbatical cycle can be synchronized. Whatever the Torah's understanding, there can be no doubt that texts of the Second Temple period understand the jubilee as a forty-nine-year period. One such work is the Book of Jubilees, from sometime in the second half of the second century BCE, in which the jubilee cycle plays such a prominent role that scholars have named the book after it. Although Jubilees presents itself as a revelation from the angel of the presence to Moses, it is not usually considered an apocalypse because the revelation consists of a reworking of the Torah's narrative from creation through the exodus from Egypt in light of Jubilees' special concerns. The book dates all the events it recounts according to jubilees of forty-nine years. The exodus and Israel's entrance into the land take place in the fiftieth jubilee from the creation of the world; thus the fiftieth jubilee is a time of liberty like the fiftieth year of the jubilee cycle. The narrative of Jubilees concludes with the exodus and offers no predictions about the eschaton, but it would be appropriate, symmetrical, and not entirely implausible chronologically given the date of Jubilees' composition to see the exodus and entrance into the land as the midpoint of world history, with history to conclude in the 100th jubilee. An explicitly eschatological interpretation of the law of the jubilee year appears in a fragmentary text from the Dead Sea Scrolls, 11QMelchizedek, which dates the eschaton to the tenth jubilee; it is not clear when the ten jubilees begin. It is also worth noting that the Apocryphon of Jeremiah (4Q390), another fragmentary text from the Scrolls, refers to both a jubilee and a period of seventy years in the course of its review of history and prophecy of the end.

In the wake of the destruction of the Second Temple in 70 CE, 4 Ezra and 2 Baruch continue to treat seven as a significant number, but they prefer to divide history into twelve periods. 4 Ezra places its hero halfway through the ninth period (4 Ezra 14:11–12); its readers could thus understand themselves as living much closer to the end, which fits its claim, to be discussed in the next chapter, that Rome is the kingdom represented by Daniel's fourth beast. 2 Baruch, in contrast, places the disaster Baruch is experiencing, the destruction of the First Temple, in the eleventh period (2 Baruch 67:1), so close to the end of the twelve periods as to suggest that the author is speaking over the head of Baruch to address his audience, which has recently lived through the destruction of the Second Temple.

I do not know how to explain the preference for twelve over multiples of seven in 4 Ezra and 2 Baruch. But all of the schemata discussed here share the view that history is not a random succession of events with no discernible goal. Rather, though disaster may follow disaster, the course of history was long ago determined and its time measured out, and even as they wrote, the apocalyptic authors believed, it was nearing its end.

Daniel and Prophecy

The prophets of Israel's past heard God's word and conveyed it to their people. Except for the last unit of the book (Daniel 10–12), God's message comes to Daniel not through direct speech but through interpretation. The traditional stories of the first half of the book depict Daniel as a professional wise man who comes to prominence because of his skill as an interpreter of dreams; the same skill permits him to interpret the mysterious writing on the wall. As we have seen, with the emergence of an authoritative text at the center of Judaism, interpretation becomes a central religious activity. But interpretation as it is practiced in the book of Daniel is itself a species of revelation. Daniel's own interpretations

are inspired; indeed Nebuchadnezzar requires his wise me
him not only the interpretation of his dream but the dream i.
Daniel succeeds after the other wise men have failed because he
has access to the only true source of knowledge and interpretation, God. In the second portion of the book, however, Daniel
becomes a recipient of interpretation rather than an interpreter,
and the interpreter is an angel; the fact that the interpreter is an
angel serves to guarantee that the interpretation is divinely
authorized.

It is also noteworthy that when the last unit of the book aban-
dons interpretation for more direct revelation, the revealer is not
God himself, but the angel Gabriel, the same angel who served as
the interpreter of the visions in the preceding units. The fact that
Gabriel serves as both interpreter and revealer suggests that for
the book of Daniel there is not much difference between interpretation and more direct revelation. In this unit, the longest in
the book of Daniel, Gabriel describes the course of history
inscribed in the heavenly writing, with the bulk of attention to
the events through which Daniel's audience was living and the
imminent end of history. The account includes a powerful but
compressed expression of the book of Daniel's view that events
on earth are merely a reflection of the real struggle, which takes
place in heaven: Gabriel explains to Daniel that he comes to him
fresh from the battle against the angel of Persia, which he has left
in Michael's hands (Dan. 10:12–13).

The Persecution of Antiochus and the Imminence
of the End

The Book of the Watchers ranges widely over topics from the
origins of evil to the heavenly temple to the wonders of nature
and mythic geography even as it responds to the wrongdoing of
some contemporary priests. The focus of the book of Daniel is
much narrower. All four units of the apocalyptic portion of the
book are concerned with the events surrounding the Maccabean
Revolt, described in veiled terms appropriate to the setting of the
visions in Babylonia in the years just before and after the Persian

conquest. The author of Daniel clearly understood these events as a time of unprecedented crisis, the last days before God visits retribution on Israel's persecutors and inaugurates the kingdom of the holy ones. Given the repeated insistence that the real battle is being fought in heaven, it is perhaps not surprising that the imminence of the end of history is not understood as a summons to rise up against Israel's oppressors. Indeed, if the author alludes to the Maccabees at all, he considers their armed revolt only "a little help"; the real heroes of the eschatological troubles are the men of understanding who teach the people even as some of them die for their piety (Dan. 11:33–5; quotation, 11:34). In the Book of Dreams, in contrast, Judah Maccabee is depicted as a sheep that grows a great horn and holds off the birds of prey that attack it until the angel who oversees the shepherds and records their misdeeds comes to his aid. As the battle continues and the horn is in danger, God himself intervenes on the side of the sheep; they are given a sword and proceed to rout their enemies (1 Enoch 89:9–19).

When the prophets of the period of the First Temple chastised their listeners for mistreating the poor or worshiping other gods, they promised that God would forgive them if they repented and would avert the catastrophes looming on the horizon. But despite its reverence for the piety of the wise, the book of Daniel does not preach repentance. For Daniel, the course of history had been determined far in the past, and there is no room for repentance to change that course. Although it is clearly desirable to be among the righteous at the fast-approaching time of the end, the book passes up the opportunity to extol the benefits of repentance. Perhaps this is because it usually views the people of Israel as a single entity, without any distinction between sinners and pious, as in the first apocalyptic vision (Daniel 7), where the holy ones of the Most High are understood in national terms as the people of Israel, not as the righteous of Israel; though some prophetic texts distinguish a righteous remnant from the mass of sinners, the attribution of a single fate to the entire people has ample precedent in the Torah and some of the prophets.

The concluding revelation of Daniel takes a somewhat different approach to the people of Israel. Its heroes, as noted above, are the wise, who play a crucial role in the events leading up to the eschaton. It also refers to "men of violence among you people" (Dan. 11:14) in the early stages of the history it rec and to "those who forsake the holy covenant" (Dan. 11:30 "those who violate the covenant" (Dan. 11:32) in the e\ ... closer to the moment the author is writing. But in contrast to the prophetic concept of the remnant, the majority of the people are viewed as students of the wise: "And those among the people who are wise shall make many understand" (Dan. 11:33). In other words, for the crucial events of the end of history Daniel views wicked Jews as a minority and sees the mass of the people as inclining toward the good under the tutelage of the wise. This description, if not exactly a call to repentance, at least encourages its readers to follow the lead of the wise.

Life After Death

As the last stages of the eschatological drama unfold, the angel Gabriel informs Daniel about the fate of those who have already died: "Many of those who sleep in the dust of the earth shall awake, some to everlasting life, and some to shame and everlasting contempt" (Dan. 12:2). This is the first passage in the Hebrew Bible that clearly embraces the idea of an afterlife of reward and punishment though it is not the first in Jewish literature: as we have seen, the Book of the Watchers had already described a final judgment that would include the souls of all the departed. It is striking that, unlike the Book of the Watchers, Daniel does not envision resurrection for all the dead but only for some of them: "many of those who sleep in the dust ...."

The key to making sense of this limited resurrection may lie in the verse that follows: "And those who are wise shall shine like the brightness of the firmament; and those who turn many to righteousness, like the stars for ever and ever" (Dan. 12:3). Daniel's concern, then, is clearly with the righteous, some of whom suffered in a particularly public way in the course of the revolt. The problem of the suffering of the righteous was not new in the second century BCE, but the persecution that caused the Maccabean Revolt created conditions in which the righteous suffered precisely because they were righteous, that is, because they insisted on continuing to observe the laws of the Torah despite their prohibition. The fate of the martyrs is central to 2 Maccabees' account of the revolt, and 1 Maccabees mentions the sad fate of women who insisted on circumcising their sons.

But Daniel is also interested in the fate of the wicked, or at least some of the wicked: "some to shame and everlasting contempt" (Dan. 12:2). Perhaps Daniel's goal is to provide recompense to all who did not receive appropriate recompense in this life, to the wicked who flourished as well as to the righteous who suffered. In this understanding, life after death functions to right wrongs. Thus the wicked who suffered in this life and the righteous who flourished are not in need of it.

In the years following the Maccabean Revolt, the idea of life after death, either in a resurrected body on a renewed earth or in a spiritual body or astral form in heaven, as for Daniel's wise, became widespread among Jews. By early in the Common Era it had become a central tenet of both Judaism and Christianity, and the fate of souls after death becomes an important theme of apocalyptic literature, as we shall see in chapters 5 and 6.

Chapter 4

The Heavenly Messiah

It did not take long for history to prove the book of Daniel wrong: the persecution of Antiochus was not the final cataclysm before the end. Though the Temple had been cleansed of the idolatry of the Greeks and sovereignty restored to the people of Israel after four centuries of foreign rule, these momentous deeds were accomplished by the Maccabees, who hardly figure in Daniel's visions. At first, even after freeing themselves from the nominal Seleucid rule that continued after the success of the revolt, the Hasmoneans – the family that bore the epithet Maccabee during the revolt – ruled as high priests in continuity with the structure of the Judean polity under Persian and Hellenistic rule. Yet though they were priests the family had no traditional claim to high-priestly office. Their propaganda attempted to solve this problem by representing them as the spiritual, and perhaps even physical, heirs of Phinehas, the grandson of Aaron and founder of the high-priestly line (1 Macc. 2:26, 54). Whether or not their subjects were persuaded by this claim, they must have found the success of the Hasmoneans in expanding the borders of Judea and enriching it to be strong arguments in favor of their rule. Eventually the Hasmoneans began to call themselves kings as well as high priests, though as priests they could not possibly claim descent from David, the founder of the dynasty that had ruled Judah until the Babylonian conquest brought an end to the monarchy.

Despite the Hasmoneans' successes, no one was likely to confuse the state they ruled from 152 to 63 BCE with Daniel's kingdom of the holy ones of the Most High. Indeed, Hasmonean rule created the conditions that led some pious Jews to reject the rest of the Jewish people and to see themselves alone as constituting the true Israel. For the success of the Maccabean Revolt proved to be profoundly destabilizing. During the preceding centuries both the Torah and the Temple had benefited from the patronage of foreign rulers, whose power tended to keep internal disputes from intensifying to the point of sectarianism. The Hasmoneans were not constrained by foreign rulers. Nor, though they were priests, did they belong to the traditional Jewish elite; they came not from Jerusalem but from a village some distance away. Under the Hasmoneans, for the first time in Jewish history as far as we can tell, the proper way to run the Temple became the subject of heated argument. Disagreements about such crucial matters as the correct understanding of the purity laws and the festival calendar led some pious Jews to refuse to make use of the Temple altogether on the grounds that it had been defiled by the mistaken practices of the priests who ran it. While we have seen the Book of the Watchers criticize the behavior of priests, such criticism had never before escalated to the point of the sectarianism we find in the Dead Sea Scrolls.

The Dead Sea Scrolls

As noted earlier, a sect is a group that claims to have exclusive access to the truth and views everyone outside the sect as lost. The Dead Sea Scrolls, as we have seen, are the library of a group that understood its members as children of light and all others, both Jews and gentiles, as children of darkness. The library includes works written by the sect itself and works that the sect valued, including all of the books that came to form the Hebrew Bible (with the exception of the book of Esther) and other works such as the Book of the Watchers, other portions of 1 Enoch, and the Book of Jubilees. Most scholars believe that the group responsible for the Scrolls should be identified with the Essenes described by Josephus in his account of Jewish sects; both Josephus and the Scrolls indicate that some Essenes lived in families among other Jews while a small group of men lived communally at Qumran on the shores of the Dead Sea, where the Scrolls were discovered.

It is clear from the scrolls composed by the sectarians themselves that they lived in intense anticipation of the end of days. But though the sect made copies of a number of apocalypses, it did not compose apocalypses of its own. It did, however, develop its own form of eschatologically oriented scriptural exegesis, the *pesher* (plural *pesharim*). These commentaries take their name from the term meaning "interpretation," which they use to connect their exegesis to the scriptural lemma. The *pesharim* interpret scriptural prophecies as well as other passages as applying to the sect's history and to its role in the fast-approaching end of days:

A particularly vivid picture of the sect's expectations about the end of days emerges from the War Scroll, a "rule," in the terminology of the Scrolls, for the battles between the children of light and the children of darkness at the end of days. Other rules among the Scrolls order the communal life of sectarians living at Qumran (the Community Rule), the lives of members of the sect living among other Jews (the Damascus Covenant), and the future communal life of sectarians in the eschaton (the Rule of the Congregation). Fighting alongside the children of light, according to the War Scroll, are the angels of light. The children of darkness are assisted in battle by the forces of Belial, the Scrolls' preferred name for the head of the evil angels. First one side is victorious and then the other in three sets of battles, until God himself gives victory to the forces of light. The scroll makes it clear that these are no ordinary battles. The war rages for decades, but the forces of light cease fighting during sabbatical years. Their trumpets, standards, and javelins are inscribed with slogans of trust in God, and they make use of swords and shields fashioned of precious metals and jewels. The soldiers are to be 40 to 50 years of age, surely well past the military prime, while the supply troops who also clear the battlefield of the dead are 25 to 30 years of age. The manner of battle may reflect Roman military practice, but such real-world influences are subordinated to ideas about holy war rooted in Scripture, from Deuteronomy's rules for eliminating from the army all who are not whole-hearted to Joshua's tactics in the course of the conquest of the Promised Land.

The hero of the eschatological battles laid out in the War Scroll is not a human leader but God himself, whom the scroll addresses thus: "Rise up, hero, take your captives, man of glory, and take your spoil, valiant one" (col. 12.10–11). But the War Scroll does mention in passing the human leaders, the high priest and the prince of the whole congregation; both titles are known from other texts among the Dead Sea Scrolls as well. These figures should probably be identified with the two messianic figures known from elsewhere in the Scrolls, the messiah of Aaron, a high priest, and the messiah of Israel, sometimes identified as a descendant of David. The texts in which the two messiahs appear have rather little to say about the function of these figures. The most extended description is probably the one in the Rule of the Congregation. It shows the messiah of Israel together with a priest who is not actually called a messiah presiding at the meals of the community in time to come (col. 2.11–22). Furthermore, the titles are just that, titles; there is no mention of actual figures filling them. And while a two-messiah scheme is the dominant one in the Scrolls, it is not the only one. Several texts refer to only a single messiah, the Davidic king, though in most cases the discussion appears in the course of exegesis of a passage about a descendant of David and so should not be taken to exclude the existence of a priestly messiah. Finally, there are several texts among the Scrolls that refer to an eschatological prophet, sometimes juxtaposed with the messiahs of Aaron and Israel.

One aspect of the War Scroll's scenario that should be emphasized is the cooperation it envisions between human and angelic forces in the eschatological battles. Other scrolls reflect the sectarians' belief that they lived in the company of angels even in the present. In one sense the Book of the Watchers goes further by claiming that Enoch is actually superior in status to many of the angels, but the Scrolls make their claim for communion with the angels not for a single pious hero but for the entire sectarian community. Some of the ascent apocalypses discussed in the next chapter take up the question of the relationship of a group of human beings to the angels, but the group in question is not an earthly community but the righteous after death.

Roman Rule

In 63 BCE the Romans, by then the major power in the eastern Mediterranean, intervened in a civil war between two Hasmonean brothers, and a century of Judean independence came to an end; Judea was to remain under Roman rule until the Muslim conquest in 638 CE. The Jews clearly found the Romans more difficult overlords than their predecessors had been. Perhaps the century of independence would have made any new rulers harder to bear, but the way the Romans ruled their empire also contributed to the difficulties, for it left subject peoples open to abuse from rapacious governors who had taken their posts in the hope of making their fortunes as quickly as possible, a hazard less pronounced under the Persians or the Hellenistic empires. In addition, the Romans, who usually tried to enlist the help of the local elite in governing their subject peoples, found the Jewish elite a particularly bad fit. The Romans were used to dealing with military aristocracies, with whom they had something in common. The hereditary aristocracy of Judea consisted primarily of priests whose prestige came not from military prowess but from their relationship to the Temple and the Torah. At first the Romans ruled Judea as a semi-autonomous kingdom with a local dignitary, the infamous Herod, as its ruler. Herod was not a native Judean, but an Idumean who had adopted Judaism and who had close ties to the Hasmonean family, including a wife who was a Hasmonean princess. This relationship might have contributed to legitimizing Herod in the eyes of subjects attached to the Hasmoneans had he not proceeded to kill off his brother-in-law, his wife, and eventually his sons by her as well, leaving only his young grandsons to carry on the Hasmonean line. The unhappiness of Herod's subjects was reflected in the regular disturbances that took place under him.

Herod died in 4 BCE, and his kingdom was divided among his surviving sons. In 6 CE the Romans began to rule directly through governors, known first as prefects and later as procurators, and tensions only increased. Official Roman practice was sensitive to the eccentricities of the Jews. It permitted them to observe the Sabbath and it did not insist on sacrifice to the emperor, now treated as divine, but accepted instead twice-daily sacrifices in the Jerusalem Temple on behalf of the emperor and Rome; while gold and silver coins with the emperor's image circulated in Judaea, the image did not appear on the copper coins that were actually minted there. But official tolerance did not spare the Jews the greed of some of their governors, nor did it prevent disturbances when Roman soldiers enraged the population by publicly mocking their customs.

Popular discontent with Roman rule in Judea was evident well before the events that led up to Jewish revolt of 66–70 CE in the series of uprisings, small and of brief duration, on which Josephus, the first-century historian of the Jews, reports with considerable distaste. Many of these uprisings were led by aspiring kings or by prophets predicting the imminent end of Roman rule and perhaps of history itself. I will have more to say about them later in the chapter. The sectarians of the Dead Sea Scrolls, in contrast, maintained their intense eschatological expectations for generations without engaging in rebellion as they awaited the final showdown between the children of light and the children of darkness. Later in this chapter I will discuss the picture of the messiah in the book of Revelation, a product of the most important ancient Jewish movement that followed a prophet predicting the imminent end of history, the early Jesus movement. Although Jesus does not seem to have participated in rebellion or even advocated it, the Romans appear to have understood him as another dangerous rabble-rouser.

According to Josephus these uprisings attracted only the poor and uneducated. Though this picture may reflect Josephus' hostility rather than their actual demographics, what we know about the earliest followers of Jesus does suggest that the people involved in these movements did not share the high level of literacy and learning reflected in the Dead Sea Scrolls. But whatever the make-up of the pre-66 rebellions, there can be no doubt that the revolt of 66–70 began with support from all elements of

Jewish society. The revolt broke out after a particularly vicious attack by the Romans on unarmed civilians aroused popular anger and led the priests to stop the daily sacrifice on behalf of Rome and the emperor. The cessation of this sacrifice amounted to a declaration of war. The rebels managed to hold out for four years, longer than could have been expected against the might of Rome, but the rebellion ended in disaster with the destruction of the Second Temple and much of the city of Jerusalem.

Just as the Maccabean Revolt inspired the composition of Daniel and the Book of Dreams, the fall of Jerusalem and the destruction of the Temple inspired the writing of several apocalypses: 4 Ezra, 2 Baruch, the Apocalypse of Abraham, and 3 Baruch. But unlike Daniel and the Book of Dreams, which were written in the midst of the Maccabean Revolt, these apocalypses were written some time after the rebellion had been suppressed as Jews, and perhaps Christians as well, attempted to make sense of the devastation caused by the revolt. The Apocalypse of Abraham and 3 Baruch will be treated together with other apocalypses involving ascent to heaven in the next chapter. In this chapter I will focus on 4 Ezra in particular because of its strong and distinctive voice, but I will also consider 2 Baruch and the Parables of Enoch (1 Enoch 37–71), an apocalypse written somewhat earlier, probably early in the period of Roman rule, with important points of contact with the later works. I will also discuss the book of Revelation, dating from some time in the first century CE, the only apocalypse to become part of the New Testament.

4 Ezra

4 Ezra is set in the aftermath of the destruction of the First Temple; the enemy whose victory Ezra laments is Babylon rather than Rome. As we have seen, the historical Ezra was active more than a century after the destruction of the First Temple; he served the Persians, who had defeated the Babylonians. Though the historical details of the Persian period were not well known to the author of the book of Daniel, it seems unlikely that the author of

4 Ezra actually believed Ezra to have been an eyewitness to the destruction of the First Temple. More likely he was drawn to Ezra as the "scribe skilled in the Torah of Moses" (Ezra 7:6; my trans.), the moving force in the communal reform and restoration more than a century after the destruction, whose career is described in the biblical book that bears his name. He was apparently prepared to sacrifice historical accuracy to the message of hope implicit in his comparison of the destruction of the Second Temple with that of the First: seventy years after the destruction of the First Temple, the Second Temple was dedicated. The same implicit comparison of First and Second Temples appears in 2 Baruch. Here the fit is smoother than in 4 Ezra since the historical Baruch, the scribe of the prophet Jeremiah, lived through the destruction of the First Temple. It is noteworthy that, like Enoch, both heroes are scribes.

Though its original language was probably Hebrew, 4 Ezra reached the West in Latin by way of a Greek translation now lost but attested by daughter translations into a variety of eastern languages, such as Georgian and Armenian. With the possible exception of the Greek, all of these translations were made by and for Christians, and the scribes who copied 4 Ezra were Christians. Thus, as discussed in chapter 1, it is not surprising that Christian elements entered the work at different stages. At one point where the texts of the other versions read "my son, the messiah," the Latin reads "my son Jesus"; clearly "Jesus" did not form part of the original form of the work but was added by a scribe either consciously or unconsciously clarifying the identity of the messiah. A more ambitious effort at Christianizing the Latin version of 4 Ezra can be seen in the brief, independent apocalypses attributed to Ezra placed at its beginning and end to form the work known in English collections of the Apocrypha as 2 Esdras; in light of the other versions it is clear that these portions are later additions. 2 Esdras 1–2 is known to scholars as 5 Ezra, while 2 Esdras 15–16 is known as 6 Ezra. The text referred to here as 4 Ezra corresponds to 2 Esdras 3–14. 4 Ezra is thus in the strange position of beginning with chapter 3.

4 Ezra is a carefully structured work that consists of seven units: three dialogues between Ezra and the angel Uriel in which Ezra

laments the unjust fate of his people (4 Ezra 3:1–5:19, 5:20–6:34, 6:35–9:25), a pivotal vision that transforms Ezra's view of the world (4 Ezra 9:26–10:59), two visions of the coming end (4 Ezra 11–12, 13), and finally a scene in which Ezra acts as a second Moses, dictating anew the books first revealed to Moses as well as seventy more (4 Ezra 14). Each unit is separated from the next by seven days, except for the fifth unit, the first eschatological vision, which comes the day after the transformative vision that precedes it, and the final revelation, which comes three days after the vision that precedes it. After each unit, Ezra's angelic interlocutor tells him how to prepare for the next vision; the preparation includes fasting (after the first two dialogues) and eating flowers in the field (after the third dialogue and the first eschatological vision), but also simply staying put (after the transformative vision and the second eschatological vision).

The Dialogues in 4 Ezra

How can God allow his own people, for whose sake he created the world, to suffer so much? This question is the starting point for the dialogues between Ezra and the angel Uriel. Ezra admits that Israel has sinned, but, after all, it is God who created human beings with their wicked hearts, as Adam's sinfulness demonstrates. Furthermore, though Israel failed to obey the laws of the Torah, the Babylonians are surely no better, and yet having conquered and oppressed Israel they continue to prosper. Uriel defends God's justice. He begins by reprimanding Ezra for thinking that he can understand God's ways: those who dwell on earth should restrict themselves to earthly matters; heavenly matters are outside their sphere. Ezra rejects this line of argument, insisting that the fate of Israel is in fact an earthly matter. It is remarkable to find an apocalypse insisting that human beings should not meddle in heavenly matters. The view that there are proper limits on human inquiry appears also in some works from the Wisdom tradition such as Job and the Wisdom of ben Sira, but it stands in sharp contrast to the view of most of the apocalypses, in which seers ascend to heaven or have heavenly mysteries revealed to them. It seems that 4 Ezra is criticizing their claims.

Uriel goes on to insist that though the number of the righteous is small, the blessed fate they will enjoy after death and in the world to come demonstrates God's righteousness. Ezra is not satisfied. The end is too long in coming, and though Uriel assures Ezra that he is among the righteous, there is little comfort in the angel's words for the majority of Israel, who will never enjoy the rewards of the righteous. Uriel argues that sin is a matter of human choice: Israel was warned and should have obeyed. "The Most High made this world for the sake of many, but the world to come for the sake of the few ... Many have been created, but few shall be saved" (4 Ezra 8:1, 3). Ezra finds this picture of the fate of humanity unbearable and prays to God to show mercy to the people of Israel. The third dialogue concludes with Ezra still unsatisfied, as his last words show: "I said before, and I say now, and will say it again: there are more who perish than those who will be saved, as a wave is greater than a drop of water" (4 Ezra 9:15–16).

The only other apocalypse to make extensive use of dialogue is the contemporary work 2 Baruch. It is preserved in Syriac, probably translated from a Greek version that survives in fragments, which probably goes back to a now lost Hebrew original. The concluding portion of the work was quite popular, but the work as whole survives in only a single manuscript, a fact that reminds us how much our knowledge of the apocalypses depends on chance. As in 4 Ezra, the dialogues in 2 Baruch give Baruch the opportunity to lament the fate of Israel (2 Baruch 1–52). Baruch's interlocutor is God himself rather than an angel, but his lament covers the same subjects as Ezra's – the triumph of gentiles over Israel – and even includes a number of more detailed similarities, such as the sin of Adam as an indication of the difficulty of doing right for human beings and emphasis on right and wrong as human choice. These similarities, together with similarities in setting and structure, have persuaded many scholars that the works are in some way related, though there does not appear to be direct dependence of one on the other. But the similarities also serve to underline the distinctive character of 4 Ezra. While Baruch is apparently satisfied with the answers he receives from God, dropping each subject as God responds to him, Ezra repeatedly refuses to accept the angel's assurances about God's justice, questioning him again after each response. Not until the vision that makes up the fourth unit is Ezra willing to accept the angel's arguments.

Ezra's Transformation

After the third dialogue, at the angel's command, Ezra goes out into a field, eats flowers for a week, and prays again, again lamenting the fate of Israel. As he is praying he sees a woman in mourning. The woman tells Ezra that her only son, born to her after thirty years of barrenness, died as he entered the wedding chamber on the day set for his marriage. So great is her grief that she plans to fast and mourn until she dies. Upon hearing her words Ezra becomes angry:

> You most foolish of women, do you not see our mourning and what has happened to us? For Zion, the mother of us all, is in deep grief and affliction ... Keep your sorrow to yourself, and bear bravely the troubles that have come upon you. For if you acknowledge the decree of God to be just, you will receive your son back in due time, and will be praised among women. (4 Ezra 10:6–7, 15–16)

But the woman refuses to stop her mourning and insists that she will remain in the field until she dies.

Ezra tries again to make the woman see it his way, this time by giving her an elaborate list of the sorrows that have befallen Jerusalem. As he concludes, urging her to stop mourning and await God's mercy, the woman begins a terrifying transformation. She cries out, the earth shakes, and where the woman had stood, there stands instead a huge city of beautiful appearance. As Ezra falls on the ground in fear, Uriel returns and explains that the woman is Zion and the story she told of her loss is the story of the destruction of Jerusalem. The woman's transformation is Ezra's reward for his effort to comfort her: "For now the Most High, seeing that you are sincerely grieved and profoundly distressed for her, has shown you the brilliance of her glory, and the loveliness of her beauty" (4 Ezra 10:50). Finally Uriel promises Ezra that he will show him the fate of those living at the end of days (4 Ezra 10:57); these visions make up the next two units of the work.

Like the woman, Ezra undergoes a transformation in the course of this vision, though his transformation is psychological rather than physical. In his dialogues with Uriel Ezra remained unyielding, continuing to complain of God's treatment of his people despite Uriel's arguments and promises of consolation, yet in this vision he attempts to comfort the mourning woman with the hope that God will restore her son to her. There is a certain irony in Ezra's offering advice he has himself rejected, but the change in outlook is psychologically plausible. Upon finding himself in the role Uriel had played with him, Ezra finally comes to embrace Uriel's point of view.

Rewriting the Bible

It is only after this transformation that Ezra receives the two visions that describe the messiah and the events of the eschaton. I shall turn to those visions and the relationship of their picture of the messiah and the eschatological drama to that of other works shortly. First I would like to consider briefly the concluding unit of 4 Ezra. In this unit Ezra drinks a cup filled with a fiery liquid and proceeds to dictate day and night for forty days to five scribes; the dictation results in ninety-four books. Twenty-four of them are to be made public; these presumably are the books that make up the Hebrew Bible. The other seventy are to be given "to the wise among your people" (4 Ezra 14:46); presumably 4 Ezra itself is one of these. This remarkable passage helps to explain the existence of the text of 4 Ezra itself, and it also heightens Ezra's prestige by making him a second Moses. Ezra is able to receive the revelations about the future in the fifth and sixth units only after he has come to accept that God's treatment of Israel is just and right. In the final unit he goes even further, becoming the vehicle for God's communication of his will to the entire people as well as of the teachings reserved for the wise.

The Fourth Kingdom Revisited

I now turn back to the fifth and sixth units of 4 Ezra, the eschatological visions Uriel bestows on Ezra after his encounter with the mourning woman. In keeping with Ezra's transformation as a result of that encounter, these visions are interpreted by God himself.

The first of the visions is of an eagle with three heads and twelve wings that rises up out of the sea to rule over the whole earth. After each of the twelve wings has ruled or attempted to rule, several additional little wings attempt to rule the earth. But the middle head, the greatest of the heads, brings the wings under control and rules the whole earth until it too disappears, leaving the two smaller heads in command until the head on the right devours the head on the left. At this point a lion appears and addresses the eagle, identifying it as the fourth beast to rule over the world and warning it that God is about to destroy it for its arrogance. As Ezra watches, the head disappears, two wings rise and fall, and the body of the eagle is burned.

God's interpretation of the vision makes clear what the lion's speech hints at: "The eagle which you saw coming up from the sea is the fourth kingdom which appeared in a vision to your brother Daniel. But it was not explained to him as I now explain ..." (4 Ezra 12:11). The final beast of Daniel's vision represented the Greek dynasties that followed Alexander, culminating in the arrogant small horn, Antiochus IV. But, as the author of 4 Ezra and his audience knew all too well, the terrible fourth beast of Daniel 7 was not the last empire to rule over Israel. Though the identities of the various wings and heads are not obvious, at least to modern readers, the use of the eagle on the standards of the Roman army made it an unmistakable and threatening symbol of the Roman empire. In other words, Ezra's vision updates Daniel's prophecy of the four kingdoms much as the interpretation Daniel receives from Gabriel updates Jeremiah's prophecy of seventy years of punishment.

The author of 4 Ezra was not the only apocalyptic author impressed by the vision of the four kingdoms. The book of Revelation (Revelation 13) describes a beast that combines characteristics of all four of the beasts Daniel saw: its mouth is like a lion, the first of Daniel's beasts; its feet are like a bear's, the second of Daniel's beasts; its overall likeness is to a leopard, the third of Daniel's beasts; and it has ten horns, like the fourth beast. This beast shares the stage with another beast that comes out of the earth and with the dragon of the previous vision that ranks higher than the two beasts and confers authority on them.

2 Baruch also provides a strong indication of the prestige of the idea of four kingdoms. There is no obvious connection between the four-kingdoms schema and Baruch's vision of a great forest that is eventually overcome by a stream and a vine, but the interpretation reads the vision in terms of that schema: the great forest represents the fourth kingdom, the single surviving cedar stands for the last ruler of that kingdom, and the stream and vine represent the kingdom of the messiah (2 Bar. 36–9).

The One Like a Son of Man in the Parables of Enoch

As these adaptations of Daniel 7 show, the fourth kingdom was the focus of more interest than the previous three kingdoms. This is not surprising. The fourth kingdom, after all, was the kingdom under which the apocalyptic authors believed themselves and their contemporaries to be suffering. But the ultimate concern of all of these apocalypses is what follows the fourth kingdom, the kingdom represented in Daniel 7 by the one like a son of man riding the clouds of heaven.

The earliest apocalypse to preserve an interpretation of the figure is the Parables of Enoch, a work preserved only in Ethiopic as part of 1 Enoch (chapters 37–71) that probably dates from the first century BCE. This difficult work consists of three visions of the eschatological fate of the righteous and of the wicked who oppress them. Most of the revelation takes place in the divine throne room, familiar from the Book of the Watchers and Daniel. Central to the eschatological drama is a figure most often referred to as the "son of man" or the "chosen one"; the terms occur with almost equal frequency, usually in distinct portions of the text. Another designation used for this figure also deserves mention, although it appears only twice: anointed one or messiah (1 Enoch 48:10, 52:4); I shall return to it below.

Just as in Daniel 7 the one like a son of man receives dominion from the white-haired Ancient of Days, who sits in the midst of his divine courtiers on a fiery throne with books open before him (Dan. 7:9–10), the son of man in the Parables is the agent of the white-haired Head of Days (1 Enoch 46:1 etc.), who sits on a throne of glory surrounded by his angels with the books of the living open before him (1 Enoch 47:3–4). In Daniel 7, the career of the figure of human appearance is limited to arriving on the clouds and accepting rule from the Ancient of Days. In contrast, the figure in the Parables is an important actor in the eschatological drama. He is to punish the kings and the mighty of the earth for their arrogance and their persecution of the righteous (1 Enoch 46:4–8, 48:8–9, etc.), and his deeds and attributes are described in some detail: he supports the righteous (1 Enoch 48:4–5), he is full of wisdom (1 Enoch 49:3–4, 51:2–5), and he will preside at the Last Judgment (1 Enoch 62).

The Parables' picture of the son of man is deeply influenced by a number of biblical passages in addition to Daniel 7, most importantly the description of the ideal Davidic king in Isaiah 11 and the servant songs of the later parts of the book of Isaiah. Like the king of Isaiah 11, the son of man of the Parables is both warrior and judge, and he performs both tasks with more than human skill. The influence of Isaiah 11 can be seen also in the language of the Parables. I quote first from Isaiah 11 and then from the Parables:

> The Spirit of the Lord shall rest upon him, the spirit of wisdom and understanding, the spirit of counsel and might, the spirit of knowledge and the fear of the LORD … He shall not judge by what his eyes see, or decide by what his ears hear, but with righteousness he shall judge the poor, and decide with equity for the meek for the earth; and he shall smite the earth with the rod of his mouth, and with the breath of his lips he shall slay the wicked. (Isa. 11:2–4)

> In him will dwell the spirit of wisdom and the spirit of insight, the spirit of instruction and might, and the spirit of those who have fallen asleep in righteousness. And he will judge the things that are secret, and a lying word none will be able to speak in his presence … (1 Enoch 49:3–4)

> The spirit of righteousness was poured upon him. And the word of his mouth will slay all sinners … (1 Enoch 62:2)

The title "son of man" plays an important role in the New Testament in dozens of sayings in the synoptic gospels and in the Gospel of John. One of its main uses is as a title for an exalted eschatological figure much like the son of man of the Parables. Thus, for example,

> And then they will see the [s]on of man coming in clouds with great power and glory. And then he will send out the angels, and gather his elect from the four winds, from the ends of the earth to the ends of heaven. (Mark 13:26–7; RSV capitalizes "Son")

It is not impossible that the gospel writers knew the Parables, but it is more likely that the understanding of the son of man as an eschatological savior was sufficiently widespread in turn-of-the-era Judaism that no direct influence is necessary to account for the presence of the term. Below we shall see the impact of the figure of the son of man on 4 Ezra, though there the figure is not called "son of man."

"Chosen One" in the Parables

The son of man of the Parables is also called the "chosen one." This name links him to the suffering servant of the later parts of the book of Isaiah, whom God calls "my chosen one" (Isa. 42:1; my trans.). Together with the biblical passages already discussed, the servant songs make an important contribution to the description of this figure. Because of its associations with the suffering servant, the name "chosen one" links the one who bears it to the suffering righteous. Indeed, the Parables frequently refers to the righteous as "the chosen" (e.g., 1 Enoch 39:6, 40:5, 50:1, 58:1–3, 62:12–13), and the chosen one is even said to choose them: "In those days, my Chosen One will arise, and choose the righteous and holy from among them" (1 Enoch 51:5a, 2). The consternation of kings and the mighty at the sight of the exaltation of the chosen one (1 Enoch 62) recalls the astonishment of the mighty at the exaltation of the servant (Isa. 52:13–15). As the chosen one is exalted, so the righteous appear to have an angelic existence in store for them:

And in that place my eyes saw the Chosen One of righteousness and faith ... and the righteous and chosen will be without number before him forever and ever. And I saw his dwelling beneath the wings of the Lord of Spirits, and all the righteous and chosen were mighty before him like fiery lights ... (1 Enoch 39:6–7)

Messiah in the Parables

The Hebrew word from which "messiah" is derived means one anointed with oil, as does the Greek "Christ." The term "messiah" originally referred to kings and priests since the Bible requires anointing for both types of officials before they assume their office, but it came to be used for a royal or priestly eschatological savior. It should also be noted that a more figurative use of the term had come into use by the time of the Babylonian exile: the prophet of Second Isaiah refers to Cyrus king of Persia as "God's messiah" (Isa. 45:1) because Cyrus is performing a mission for him.

Yet despite his identification as the messiah, a title associated with human beings, the chosen one, like the Davidic king of Isaiah 11, is surely more than human. Indeed, from one point of view his status is higher than that of the one like a son of man in Daniel 7, for in Daniel's vision only the Ancient of Days is seated while in the Parables God seats the chosen one on the throne of glory at the time of the judgment (1 Enoch 62:2–3). The Parables also asserts that the son of man was part of God's plan from the very beginning: "Even before the sun and the constellations were created, before the stars of heaven were made, his name was named before the Lord of Spirits" (1 Enoch 48:3). It even appears to claim that he was created before the world: "He was chosen and hidden in [God's] presence before the world was created" (1 Enoch 48:6). It is hard to know how to understand this claim, especially because in the concluding chapters of the Parables, Enoch learns that he is the son of man. Many scholars, it is true, view these chapters as a later addition to the Parables. Still, the identification of Enoch with a figure both human and divine, whether original or not, is not surprising in light of the Book of the Watchers' representation of Enoch as living on the boundary between the angelic and the human sphere.

Messiahs and Prophets of the End in the First Century CE

From Josephus and the New Testament we learn that first-century Judea was a place where would-be messiahs and prophets were able to assemble crowds of followers despite the likelihood of a harsh response from their rulers. John the Baptist, familiar from the gospel accounts of Jesus' baptism, was one of the earliest of these prophets, active in the 30s CE; Josephus too reports on John's activity (*Antiquities* 18.116–19). John called on his listeners to repent since God's judgment was imminent, and baptized them as a physical sign of their spiritual regeneration. The synoptic gospels attribute John's execution to his criticism of the marriage to his brother's wife of Herod Antipas, one of the sons of Herod the Great who ruled a portion of his father's kingdom after his death (Matt. 14:1–12; Mark 6:14–29; Luke 9:7–9). But Josephus suggests that John was put to death because Herod Antipas was worried about the possibility that the crowds John attracted with his preaching might rebel.

Around the year 45, Josephus reports, the prophet Theudas, who is also mentioned in the New Testament (Acts 5:36), took his followers to the Jordan and promised that the river would part to allow them to cross (*Antiquities* 20.97–8). A decade later, according to Josephus, an Egyptian prophet gathered a crowd at the Mount of Olives and promised that the walls of Jerusalem would fall at his command (*Jewish War* 2.261–3; *Antiquities* 20.169–71). Both of these prophets were claiming the mantle of Joshua, the successor of Moses, who led the children of Israel through the parted waters of the Jordan on their entrance to the Promised Land and brought down the walls of Jericho in the course of his conquest of the land. By the mid-first century Judea was under direct Roman rule, and even if the prophets' activities were nonviolent, the Romans saw them as dangerous. They responded by scattering the crowds and killing or taking captive as many as they could.

Josephus also reports the rise of several bandit-kings who gathered followings of some significance following the death of Herod at the end of the first century BCE. At least according to

Josephus, some of these men called themselves kings, an inherently messianic claim in the context of ancient Judea (*Antiquities* 17.273–85). But the most dramatic example of an anti-Roman leader acting the part of messiah comes from Simon b. Giora, one of the most important Jewish leaders during the last years of the revolt against Rome. One way he attracted followers was by offering freedom to slaves (*Jewish War* 4.508). At the end of the Roman siege of Jerusalem, when he saw that escape was impossible, he allowed himself to be captured in the ruins of the Temple dressed in white garments and a purple cape (*Jewish War* 7.29–31).

By any measure, the most important messianic figure of the first century, or indeed of any century since, was Jesus of Nazareth. Below I discuss the earliest apocalypse written by one of his followers. Here let me note only that although Jesus' post-mortem success sets him apart from the figures Josephus describes, during his lifetime a Roman observer, or indeed anyone who was not a committed follower, would probably have seen him as not very different from John or the other prophets just described.

The Messiah in 4 Ezra and 2 Baruch

As he contemplated the aftermath of the revolt against Rome, it is not surprising that the author of 4 Ezra envisioned a messiah who would take vengeance on Israel's enemies. It is also not surprising that in the wake of the failed revolt 4 Ezra's messiah is an exalted figure whose only clearly human feature is his Davidic descent (4 Ezra 12:32); the author might well have concluded that Israel's enemies would never be defeated by a human leader. The messiah appears in 4 Ezra in the two visions that follow Ezra's encounter with the woman who turns into Zion. In the first of the visions he appears as a lion that announces the demise of the eagle symbolizing Rome (4 Ezra 11:36–12:3); the lion is the symbol of Judah (Gen. 49:9), the tribe of David. In the second vision he is pictured as a man coming up out of the sea, flying on the clouds of heaven (4 Ezra 13:2–3). A multitude gathers to make war against him, but as the multitude rushes at him, he neither lifted his hand nor held a spear or any weapon of war; but I saw only how he sent forth from his mouth as it were a stream of fire, and from his lips a flaming fire, and from his tongue he shot forth a storm of sparks. All these were mingled together ... so that suddenly nothing was seen of the innumerable multitude but only the dust of ashes and the smell of smoke. (4 Ezra 13:9–11)

This messiah too appears to have been created long ago, for we are told that he has been hidden away to await the end of days (4 Ezra 12:32, 13:26).

The combination of Daniel's one like a son of man flying on the clouds and Isaiah 11's Davidic king slaying his enemies with the breath of his mouth is already familiar from the Parables. Like the chosen one of the Parables, 4 Ezra's messiah is to punish the wicked and save the remnant of Israel (4 Ezra 12:32–4, 13:25–50). He will also judge them (4 Ezra 12:33, 13:37–8), though this role is not given much emphasis.

The messiahs of 4 Ezra and the Parables play very different roles in the two works. The messiah is absolutely central to the Parables; the whole work focuses on him. The messiah in 4 Ezra is crucial to the eschatological drama, but he is much less central to the interests of the work as a whole. 4 Ezra's focus is not on the suffering of the righteous as such, but rather on Ezra's distress at the injustice of their suffering. The crucial moment in 4 Ezra is Ezra's acceptance, after having long rejected it, of the promise of future reward as a real solution to the problem.

As in 4 Ezra, the messiah in 2 Baruch plays a central role in the eschatological process but a less central role in the work as a whole. Like the chosen one of the Parables and the messiah of 4 Ezra, the messiah of 2 Baruch is preexistent, to be "revealed" (2 Baruch 29:3) when history has run its course. But in 2 Baruch, even more than in the Parables and 4 Ezra, the influence of Isaiah 11 is dominant. The messiah will judge the nations, punishing those who have harmed Israel, sparing those who have not (2 Baruch 72); he will then rule over a world in which the transformation of nature, as in Isaiah 11, permits all to live in peace and joy (2 Baruch 73, esp. 73:6).

Jesus Christ and the Book of Revelation

The earliest apocalypse by a follower of Jesus is the book of Revelation. Late twentieth-century scholarship tended to date Revelation toward the end of the first century, but recently several scholars have argued in favor of the traditional dating, which places it even earlier, under Nero, shortly before the destruction of the Temple in the year 70. John of Patmos, the author of Revelation, is unusual among the authors of apocalypses in writing in his own name rather than under the pseudonym of a biblical hero. The only other ancient apocalypse in which an author uses his own name is the work of a Christian writing in Rome in the middle of the second century, the Shepherd of Hermas. The Shepherd is unusual in other ways as well: Hermas's visions address his personal problems, and much of the work consists of exhortations and rules for leading a pious life. Despite the differences between Revelation and the Shepherd, however, it is surely significant that the authors of both works belonged to a movement that celebrated the return of prophecy in the last days; this attitude toward prophecy must have made it easier for the early followers of Jesus to accept a prophetic book written by a contemporary. The type of prophecy in which these authors engage is of course very different from that of the prophets described by Josephus, whose prophetic activity consisted of deeds rather than words.

The island of Patmos lies off the coast of Asia Minor, and John's connection to the Jesus movement in Asia Minor is evident in the "letters" to churches in seven cities of Asia Minor that preface the apocalypse proper (Revelation 1–3). It is also clear from his book that John was Jewish, and even as a follower of Jesus he appears to have remained loyal to Jewish ritual law. Recently several scholars have suggested that some of the criticism in the letters at the beginning of Revelation is directed against people who held the view of the most influential Jewish follower of Jesus, Paul, that gentile converts could dispense with Jewish ritual practices.

Yet despite their differences, John and Paul share an understanding of Jesus as an exalted heavenly being that contrasts with the synoptic gospels' picture of Jesus as a human messiah. Paul's letters, written in the 50s CE, are our earliest writings from a follower of Jesus. Of all the events in Jesus' life, Paul mentions only the crucifixion. He may have had strategic reasons for passing over Jesus' earthly career: unlike many of his apostolic competitors, he had not known Jesus during his lifetime. Still, as the Parables attests, Paul was not the first Jew to understand the messiah as a heavenly being. Indeed, Paul's picture of Christ has a great deal in common with the picture of the chosen one in the Parables and the messiah in 4 Ezra. Like them, Christ is responsible for the defeat of the wicked: "Then comes the end, when he delivers the kingdom to God the Father after destroying every rule and every authority and every power" (1 Cor. 15:24). And, like the chosen one, Christ is also the eschatological judge: "For we must all appear before the judgment seat of Christ, so that each one may receive good or evil, according to what he has done in the body" (2 Cor. 5:10; see also Rom. 2:16).

Like Paul, John was little interested in the earthly Jesus. The only clear allusion to the life of Jesus in Revelation is a reference to the crucifixion (Rev. 11:8), the same event that figures in Paul's letters. Indeed, the dominant image of Christ in the book of Revelation is not of a figure in human form but of a lamb that has been slain, with seven horns and seven eyes, an image that reflects the centrality of Christ's sacrifice in John's thought.

Like the Parables of Enoch, Revelation consists of a series of scenes that the visionary sees taking place in heaven. In Revelation, however, the visionary remains on earth, watching events unfold in heaven through an "open door" (Rev. 4:1). The events take place against the background of the liturgy of the heavenly temple, to be discussed in the next chapter. The eschatological drama begins after the death of the Lamb, or, in Revelation's description, his triumph (Rev. 5:5), that permits him to open the seven seals of a scroll of eschatological woes. As each seal is broken, another calamity or set of calamities, such as warfare, famine, and natural disasters, is unleashed on earth (Rev. 6–10). These calamities afflict all mankind, with no distinction between righteous and wicked.

Once all of the seals have been opened, John sees three loosely connected visions that share a debt to ancient Near Eastern myths of a god's defeat of a watery monster that were discussed in chapter 3. In the first such vision (Rev. 12), a dragon identified as Satan pursues a woman clothed in the sun who gives birth to a baby. The baby is taken up to God, Michael casts the dragon down to earth, and the earth opens to give the woman refuge. This vision is followed by the vision of the two beasts coming up out of the sea (Rev. 13) discussed above, which draws on Daniel 7. The vision describes the horror of the beasts and their triumph, but not their ultimate defeat. These visions are followed by an account of another set of disasters, these inflicted on the earth by angels who pour out golden bowls full of the wrath of God (Rev. 15–16). The last vision in the series is of a woman sitting upon a scarlet beast with seven heads and ten horns, "the great harlot who is seated upon many waters" (Rev. 17:1). This is "Babylon," a veiled way of referring to Rome, the Babylon of John's day. John does not recount Babylon's defeat directly, but he reports the words of the heavenly voices celebrating of her fall (Rev. 17–18).

Now, with the defeat of the forces of evil, a heavenly voice announces the wedding feast of the Lamb; the bride is later revealed to be the New Jerusalem (Rev. 19:1–10). Yet another battle is necessary before the wedding feast can take place. Until this point Christ's only contribution to the unfolding events has been his death, which set them in motion in the first place, and his blood, which purifies his followers. The eschatological woes of the seven seals and seven bowls are let loose by angels, and the only real battle against the forces of evil, the battle against the dragon, is led by the angel Michael. With the announcement of the wedding feast, however, Christ appears in a new guise, as a warrior on a white horse, with a robe that has been dipped in blood, who leads the battle against the forces of evil (Rev. 19:11–21).

Obviously a lamb would not be an appropriate leader in battle, but the new picture of Christ deserves some attention. One source for the picture is the ideal Davidic king of Isaiah 11, so important for 4 Ezra and the Parables: the "sharp sword" that comes out of Christ's mouth (Rev. 19:15) recalls the king's ability to fight the wicked with the rod of his mouth and the breath of his lips (Isa. 11:4). The blood-dipped robe derives from the prophetic picture of the divine warrior, God himself, whose garments are red with the blood of his enemies (Isa. 63:3). This imagery also reminds us that in the opening vision of the heavenly temple, before John sees the Lamb, one of the elders refers to Christ as "the Lion of the tribe of Judah, the Root of David" (Rev. 5:5). Only at the end of the work, however, does Christ manifest the characteristics associated with those titles.

Yet though Christ is no longer a lamb but a warrior, unlike the Davidic king of Isaiah 11, the chosen one of the Parables, or even the messiah of 4 Ezra, he does not serve as judge in either of the judgments that take place after the defeat of the forces of evil. After Satan is imprisoned in the pit, the martyrs preside over the first judgment, which is followed by their thousand-year reign together with Christ (Rev. 20:1–6). During the millennium, as this thousand-year period came to be known, only the martyrs have been resurrected. At the end of the thousand-year period, Satan is released from his prison and makes war on the holy ones with the help of the forces of Gog and Magog, the evil nations first mentioned in one of Ezekiel's visions of the last days (Ezek. 38:2, though there the names refer not to two nations but to a prince and his nation, "Gog of the land of Magog"). But now good triumphs forever. Fire descends from heaven to annihilate Gog and Magog, and Satan is thrown into a lake of sulfur and fire for eternal torment (Rev. 20:7–10). The second and final judgment follows, with God himself sitting alone as judge (Rev. 20:11–15). This picture echoes the picture of Daniel 7, where judgment belongs to the Ancient of Days alone. At this time all human beings receive what is due to them. Once the judgment is complete, the New Jerusalem, described in terms to be discussed in the next chapter, descends from heaven (Rev. 21:2).

Heavenly and Earthly Messiahs

Like the followers of the messianic claimants Josephus describes, the authors of apocalypses discussed in this chapter thought the end was imminent. But despite their debt to traditions about the ideal Davidic king, the authors of the apocalypses did not expect a merely human being to bring about the end of the world. Sometimes they left the task to God or an angel, but even when they envisioned a Davidic messiah, he is clearly more than human, created long ago and stored away to await the end, descending from heaven to fulfill his role. Even John of Patmos, the follower of a human messiah, is interested not in the life of Jesus of Nazareth but in his crucifixion and role as Lamb of God. The tension between John of Patmos and Paul's understanding of Christ on the one hand and that of the synoptic gospels on the other is central to Christian thought even today.

Chapter 5

The Heavenly Temple,
the Fate of Souls after Death,
and Cosmology

In the Book of the Watchers Enoch encounters God by ascending to the heavenly temple, and he learns about the punishment of the watchers, the fate of souls after death, and the wonders of nature by traveling to the ends of the earth. Though no other hero of an apocalypse journeys to the ends of the earth, ascent becomes a central mode of revelation in later apocalypses. After the turn of the era most ascent apocalypses prefer a seven-heaven schema to the single heaven of the Book of the Watchers. Seven is such a significant number as perhaps not to require explanation, though it is worth noting that Greek cosmology with its seven planetary spheres does not appear to be the source of the picture, which does not mesh well with it. Some of the ascent apocalypses use their multiple heavens to integrate into the heavens sights that Enoch sees in the course of his tour to the ends of the earth in the Book of the Watchers. But the seven-heaven schema coexists with the picture of a single heaven, which continues to appear in works from the first and second centuries of this era such as the book of Revelation and the Apocalypse of Peter, which is discussed in the next chapter.

2 Enoch

2 Enoch was probably composed in Greek, but it is preserved only in Slavonic, and the earliest manuscripts date to the fourteenth

century. Though there are few indisputably Christian elements in the work, Slavonic is a language used by Christians rather than Jews, and thus 2 Enoch is a Christian work at least in the sense that it was translated by and for Christians. On the other hand, it contains elements that cannot be explained by a medieval Slavic context, and many of these elements connect it to works of the Second Temple period. Thus, though 2 Enoch has surely undergone some development at the hands of Christian transmitters, the original form of the text, now impossible to recover, was a Jewish work from around the turn of the era.

2 Enoch begins with Enoch's ascent through the seven heavens (2 Enoch 1–10), a journey that takes the Book of the Watchers and its ascent as its point of departure and is deeply indebted to them. While it never tells the story of the descent of the watchers, 2 Enoch assumes that the reader is familiar with it when it describes the fallen watchers undergoing punishment in the second heaven while the other watchers, who did not descend, remain in the fifth heaven mourning the descent of their brethren. When Enoch arrives before the divine throne, the Lord commissions him to write an account of creation, which plays on the biblical account but differs significantly (2 Enoch 11). Then Enoch returns to earth and addresses moral advice to his children (2 Enoch 12–19). In some forms, the work concludes with an account of the transmission of priesthood from Enoch through Methuselah and Nir to Melchizedek (2 Enoch 20–3).

Like the Book of the Watchers and many other ancient Jewish and Christian works, 2 Enoch understands heaven as a temple. But it expresses this understanding somewhat differently from the Book of the Watchers. Together with many of the ascent apocalypses to be discussed in this chapter, 2 Enoch understands the heavens as the scene of liturgical activity. Until the destruction of the Temple in 70 CE, the primary Jewish cultic activity was animal sacrifice, and even after the destruction it was many decades before Jews came to recognize that the Temple would not soon be replaced. Sacrifice is a difficult activity to transfer to heaven, for obvious reasons. Some ancient texts, such as 3 Baruch and the Testament of Levi, which are discussed below, and the Songs of the Sabbath Sacrifice from the Dead Sea Scrolls, do so nonetheless, but they emphasize the aroma of the sacrifices, the most ethereal aspect of a not very ethereal process, or replace the animal victims of sacrifice with the prayers or good deeds of the righteous. But most, like 2 Enoch, understand the liturgy of the heavenly temple as hymns and songs of praise. 2 Enoch shows the heavenly liturgy taking place in all but the two lowest heavens, and it emphasizes its importance by having Enoch remind the watchers of the fifth heaven to resume their praise, which they have ceased out of grief for the fallen watchers, and by depicting the heavenly liturgy as the only activity of the sixth and seventh heavens.

In the Book of the Watchers Enoch shows himself to be a true priest, a better one than the watchers who have abandoned their posts in the heavenly temple. 2 Enoch also understands Enoch as a priest, and it goes beyond the Book of the Watchers by describing the process by which he becomes one. Upon reaching the seventh heaven, the two angels who have been guiding Enoch show him the divine throne at a distance, offer some words of encouragement, and then leave Enoch to meet God on his own. Overcome by fear, Enoch falls on his face, not once as in the Book of the Watchers but twice, clearly an effort to mark Enoch's experience before the throne as even more terrifying than the one described in the Book of the Watchers. As the angel Michael lifts Enoch from his second prostration, God himself commands Michael, "Take Enoch, and take off his earthly garments, and anoint *him* with good oil, and clothe *him* in glorious garments" (2 Enoch 9:17; italics supply words not actually found in the text). The combination of anointing and glorious garments recalls the process of investiture of the high priest described in Exodus 28–9. In Exodus the high priest is dressed in his garments before his anointing. 2 Enoch's deviation from the practice prescribed by the Torah is certainly more considerate of the glorious garments, but it is not clear whether it is purposeful and, if so, what it is intended to convey. Despite these uncertainties, there can be no doubt that the point of these rituals is to make explicit Enoch's priestly status.

2 Enoch is not the first work to depict its hero undergoing priestly investiture at the hands of angels. According to the Torah,

Aaron, the founder of the priesthood, was the first to undergo the rituals of consecration described in Exodus 28–9, but two works about Levi from the centuries around the turn of the era describe the consecration of this more distant ancestor of the priesthood, the great-grandfather of Aaron. In the Testament of Levi, Levi is dressed in priestly garments, anointed, and thus consecrated as a priest by angels in the course of a vision after an ascent to heaven. The Testament of Levi forms part of the Testaments of the Twelve Patriarchs, a Christian work composed in Greek in the second century CE, later than the pre-destruction date that I would suggest for the earliest form of 2 Enoch. But at many points the Testament of Levi reworks material from Aramaic Levi, a document from the third or second century BCE. The Aramaic text is quite fragmentary, but it is clear that there too Levi is anointed by angels in the course of a vision, though no robe is mentioned; following the vision his father Jacob dresses him and consecrates him. It is thus possible that like 2 Enoch, Aramaic Levi puts anointing before dressing in priestly garments. There is some evidence for a Greek version of the Aramaic document, which may have been the immediate source of the Testament of Levi; such a translation could have influenced 2 Enoch's ascent even if the author of the ascent did not know Aramaic.

Enoch's consecration involves replacing his "earthly garments" with "glorious garments." In light of what follows, it is clear that God is not simply directing a change of clothing. The "glorious garments" transform Enoch into an angel: "I looked at myself, and I was like one of the glorious ones, and there was no apparent difference" (2 Enoch 9:19). Indeed, they transform him into an angel exalted above the other angels since God tells him that none of his angels has ever before heard the revelation he grants Enoch (2 Enoch 11:3). Enoch's new garments, then, are much like the spiritual bodies that the righteous receive after death has taken their physical bodies according to Paul (1 Cor. 15:42–50), and as we shall see shortly, several of the ascent apocalypses suggest that not only exemplary figures such as Enoch but all of the righteous dead can achieve the status of angels.

The Apocalypse of Abraham and Ascent by Song

As noted in chapter 1, the Apocalypse of Abraham is preserved only in Slavonic. Like 2 Enoch, it probably reached its current form in the Middle Ages, yet it also contains material from much earlier. Abraham's vision of history, which contains elements likely to reflect Christian editing, includes the destruction of the Second Temple, so even the earliest form of the work probably dates to sometime after 70 CE. The work begins with a narrative about how Abraham came to recognize the one God as he helped his father with his business of making and selling idols. After striking Terah's establishment with a thunderbolt, God sends an angel to take Abraham to Mount Horeb, Deuteronomy's name for Mount Sinai. Abraham arrives there after fasting for forty days and nights, as Moses does. Then Abraham offers the sacrifice described in the covenant between the pieces of Genesis 15 and ascends to heaven together with his angelic guide on the wings of a pigeon and a turtledove. As he ascends he is frightened first by the sight of men undergoing a fiery punishment and then by a fire with a terrible sound. But he endures the terror of these experiences by reciting a song of praise that the angel teaches him: "Eternal One, Mighty One, Holy One, El, God, Monarch, Self-begotten, incorruptible, unsullied, unborn, immaculate, immortal, self-perfect, self-illumined ... Thou art he whom my soul hath loved, preserver, Eternal One" (Apoc. Abr. 17:7–8, 12). Upon reaching the seventh heaven, Abraham learns that the song he has been reciting is the song sung by the living creatures that support the divine throne, which, like the throne in the Book of the Watchers, is a version of Ezekiel's chariot (Apoc. Abr. 18:3); Ezekiel would surely have been surprised to find that once the creatures stop singing they require angelic intervention to keep them from threatening each other. The apocalypse concludes with a vision of history in which God shows Abraham the struggle of good and evil from the time of creation, through incidents familiar from the Bible, into the period that lies in the future even from the point of view of an author in the early Christian centuries. Finally Abraham returns to earth, and God promises him that he will eventually send his chosen one to save his people.

In 2 Enoch, Enoch achieves angelic status on his arrival in the seventh heaven through a process of anointing and dressing in a new garment that echoes priestly investiture. In the Apocalypse of Abraham, Abraham achieves equality with the angels by means of the song he recites, which makes him able to stand before the divine throne and converse with God. The hero's recitation of the heavenly liturgy plays a somewhat similar role in the Parables of Enoch. Though the heavenly praise does not play a role in the ascent itself, Enoch's recitation of praise and his ability to hear that of the angels (Parables 39) indicate that he belongs in heaven with nothing to fear from his proximity to the divine throne. In the concluding chapters of the Parables, Enoch's identification as the son of man is preceded by his ability to offer praise of God that goes beyond the earthly: "I fell on my face, and all my flesh melted, and my spirit was transformed. And I cried out with a loud voice, with a spirit of power, and I blessed and praised and exalted" (1 Enoch 71:11). In the following chapter we shall see that in the literature of early Jewish mysticism songs function both as a means of ascent for the visionary and as a means for the participation in the heavenly liturgy that marks his achievement of angelic status.

Angelic Garments and the Righteous Dead in the Apocalypse of Zephaniah

In the centuries before the turn of the era Jewish texts began to reflect a belief in reward and punishment after death, as we saw in the Book of the Watchers and the book of Daniel. By the turn of the era apocalypses such as the Apocalypse of Zephaniah offer a more elaborate picture of the fate of souls after death. The Apocalypse of Zephaniah survives in two manuscripts, unfortunately fragmentary, in different dialects of Coptic, the language of Christian Egypt. The name Zephaniah appears in only in one of the manuscripts, and some scholars do not accept the identification of the work in the other, more extensive, manuscript with the Apocalypse of Zephaniah. They refer to it instead as the "anonymous apocalypse."

Although the Apocalypse of Zephaniah was translated from a Greek original, its preservation in Coptic and its influence on the Apocalypse of Paul, a work composed in Egypt centuries later, make it likely that it too was composed in Egypt. Since Coptic is a language used by Christians rather than Jews, it is clear that the Coptic translation of the Apocalypse of Zephaniah was made by a Christian for Christians. Its single heaven is unusual in ascent apocalypses after the Book of the Watchers and thus possibly an indication of an early date, which would make Jewish provenance more likely. On the other hand, some of the sins attributed to the hero of the apocalypse suggest an ascetic culture appropriate to Egyptian Christianity.

The most unusual feature of the Apocalypse of Zephaniah is the identity of its hero: he is a dead soul, and his ascent to heaven takes place after his death. The hero's ultimate fate shows that he must have been righteous in life, but it seems unlikely that he is to be identified with the prophet Zephaniah, for he repeatedly shows himself to be confused and overwhelmed by the sights he encounters in the course of his heavenly journey. When he sees a sea of fire, he mistakes it for a sea of water. When a supernatural figure appears before him, he mistakes the figure for God. When he prays to be rescued, he discovers that the figure is a terrible angel, "the accuser." When his prayers for deliverance are finally answered, he mistakes the magnificent angel who has come to save him for God and attempts to worship him. While Enoch in 2 Enoch and Abraham in the Apocalypse of Abraham may be frightened by the awesome sights they encounter in heaven, they never respond the wrong way.

Yet despite his repeated failure to understand what he sees, the visionary of the Apocalypse of Zephaniah is ultimately rewarded for his good deeds. After his rescue the magnificent angel takes out a scroll on which is written every sin the visionary had committed from his childhood on. The sins are all failures of piety rather than major sins: neglecting to visit the sick, widows, and orphans, for example, or skipping fasting and prayer. The visionary prays for mercy, and an angel proclaims his victory over the accuser. The angel then unrolls a second scroll. Unfortunately we never find out what was written on this scroll since there is a gap in the manuscript, but it seems likely that it listed the hero's good deeds. Presumably this scroll was longer than the first.

When the apocalypse picks up again after two lost pages, the hero is about to be placed on a boat that carries him to paradise:

> They helped me: they set me upon the boat: they were singing praises before me, namely thousands upon thousands and myriads upon myriads of angels. I also put on an angelic garment. I saw all those angels praying. I too prayed together with them: I knew their language that they spoke with me. (Apoc. Zeph. 3:3–5)

In other words, when a soul is judged worthy to enter paradise and to be "written in the book of the living" (Apoc. Zeph. 3:8), it is given an "angelic garment." Earlier the visionary notes that the scrolls containing his deeds are written "in my own language" (Apoc. Zeph. 2:15, 3:2). But once he has put on the garment, he understands the language of the angels and is able to join in the angelic liturgy. Thus in becoming like the angels he also becomes a heavenly priest.

Yet though the soul has now achieved angelic status, it remains inferior to the highest angels:

> Then a great angel came out with a golden trumpet in his hand ... I wanted to exchange greetings with him; *but* I could not, so great was his glory. Then he hurried off to all the righteous, to Abraham, and Isaac, and Jacob, and Enoch, and Elijah, and David. He talked with them like a friend with friends ... (Apoc. Zeph. 3:6, 9–10)

The great biblical heroes, then, are the equals of the greatest angels, but our visionary, an ordinary righteous soul, is not.

Garments that confer angelic status on the righteous dead appear in several other apocalypses including the book of Revelation, which will be discussed in the next section, the Parables of Enoch, and the Apocalypse of Abraham. In the Parables, such garments are given to the righteous after the judgment of the wicked, that is, at the Last Judgment, not immediately after death:

> The righteous and the chosen will have arisen from the earth, and have ceased to cast down their faces, and have put on the garment

of glory. And this will be your garment, the garment of life from the Lord of Spirits; and your garments will not wear out, and your glory will not fade in the presence of the Lord of Spirits. (1 Enoch 62:15–16)

The angelic garment of the Apocalypse of Abraham also appears to be linked to the post-mortem fate of the righteous, although the link is not explicit. When Abraham's angelic guide recognizes the unclean bird that attempts to eat from the sacrifice Abraham has offered as Azazel, the evil angel, he rebukes him thus: "Leave this man alone ... The garment that of old was set apart in heaven for you, is *now set apart* for him" (Apoc. Abr. 13:14–15). The function of the garments in the Apocalypse of Zephaniah and the Parables suggests that Abraham's garment is meant to guarantee his angelic status after death. In light of the ability of the biblical heroes in the Apocalypse of Zephaniah, including Abraham himself, to converse with the most glorious angel, it is noteworthy that the garment promised Abraham is no ordinary angelic garment but a garment that has at one time belonged to a high-ranking angel.

The Heavenly Temple and the Righteous Dead in the Book of Revelation

Unlike the other apocalypses discussed in this chapter, Revelation does not involve an ascent to heaven. Though the book consists of a series of scenes that take place in heaven, John watches them from earth. But Revelation's picture of heaven and its understanding of the fate of the righteous dead nonetheless have much in common with those of the ascent apocalypses.

It is often claimed that early Christians rejected the Temple and its cult. John's interest in the heavenly temple makes Revelation one of many works to call this generalization into question. Whatever his attitude toward the Jerusalem Temple, and I see no reason to think it was not positive, there can be no doubt that John understands heaven as a temple. This understanding is not surprising in light of other apocalypses that hold such a view, and it fits well with John's designation of the followers of Jesus as "a kingdom, priests to his God and Father" (Rev. 1: 6), which plays on the designation of Israel as "a kingdom of priests" in the book of Exodus (Exod. 19:6).

In the course of the unfolding of the events of the end, Revelation gives us repeated glimpses of heavenly temple (Rev. 7:9–17, 11:15–19, 14:1–5, 15:1–5, 19:1–8), and the heavenly liturgy is central to its picture. The opening vision of the work describes the living creatures of Ezekiel 1, now deployed around the throne, offering praise day and night as twenty-four elders on thrones throw their crowns before the divine throne and sing their song of praise (Rev. 4: 8–11). Like the Parables, Revelation reports the words of its heavenly liturgy, drawing on biblical precedents but adding many new elements. Later in the same vision John describes the living creatures and the elders worshiping the Lamb (Rev. 5:6–14). Revelation places considerable emphasis on cultic elements of the heavenly liturgy: the elders play harps and offer golden bowls of incense consisting of the prayers of the holy ones to the Lamb, and later, after the Lamb opens the seventh seal, an angel stands at the heavenly altar with a golden censer, offering incense mingled with the prayers of the holy ones, and the smoke rises before God (Rev. 8:1–4). The heavenly temple even contains an Ark of the Covenant (Rev. 11:18).

Nor does Revelation forget about the earthly Temple. After the thousand-year reign of the Christ and the holy ones, the heavenly Jerusalem descends from heaven adorned as the bride of the Lamb (Rev. 21:1–22:5). The description of the New Jerusalem, built of gold with walls of jewels and gates of pearl, is an elaboration of imagery from Second Isaiah (Isa. 54); the river of the water of life flowing from the city comes from Ezekiel's description of the restored temple (Ezek. 47:1–12). Yet, John tells us, there is no temple in the city, "for its temple is the Lord God the Almighty and the Lamb" (Rev. 21:22). The absence of a temple in the New Jerusalem is usually read as a rejection of the Jerusalem Temple, but the identification of the temple of the New Jerusalem as God and Christ surely places a high value on it as an institution, as does John's interest in the details of the heavenly temple and its cult. And though the New Jerusalem lacks a temple building, the entire city appears to have become a temple, for John's angelic companion measures the New Jerusalem with a measuring rod (Rev. 21:15–21) just as Ezekiel's angelic guide measures the eschatological temple (Ezek. 40–2).

The righteous dead also figure prominently in John's visions. When the fifth seal is opened, John sees the souls of the martyrs, stored under the heavenly altar as they await the end, given white robes (Rev. 6:9–11). Soon after, John sees a crowd of people "from all tribes and peoples and tongues," that is, gentiles, dressed in white robes and praising God and the Lamb (Rev. 7:9–17). The activity of the righteous gentile dead, praising God and the Lamb in the heavenly temple, suggests that they are priests. Thus their white robes perform the function already familiar from the apocalypses discussed above, making the righteous dead at once angelic and priestly as they participate in the heavenly liturgy. While the acceptability of gentiles as priests is often taken as given since Revelation has reached us as part of the New Testament, it is worth dwelling on it for a moment since, as already noted, John remains loyal to Jewish ritual laws that some Jewish followers of Jesus such as Paul had already rejected. Perhaps because of this loyalty, John makes an effort to account for gentile priests before he introduces them: the song that the living creatures and the elders sing in the first vision of the heavenly temple praises the Lamb for ransoming gentiles with his blood to make them "a kingdom and priests to our God" (Rev. 5:9–10). But though John's embrace of gentiles as priests reflects his involvement in a movement in which gentiles played a central role, it is not without precedent in ancient Jewish literature: the last chapter of the book of Isaiah, which probably dates to the early Persian period, prophesies that at the end of days God will choose priests from among the gentiles to join Israel's priests (Isa. 66:21).

The righteous gentile dead are not alone as heavenly priests. Later John sees the Jewish followers of Jesus, the 144,000 from Israel who are sealed with the name of God and the Lamb, on Mount Zion with the Lamb himself, singing praise before the throne, the living creatures, and the elders (Rev. 14:1–5). Soon after, John sees the triumphant righteous, without any distinction between Jew and gentile, praising God in the heavenly temple

(Rev. 15:2–4). It is also worth noting that John calls the martyrs who reign with Christ during the millennium priests of God and Christ (Rev. 20:6).

In contrast to the heroes of the ascent apocalypses, John does not claim to have ascended to heaven. Yet at the climax of the eschatological scenario his angelic guide forbids him to bow down to him, calling himself the "fellow servant" of John and the other followers of Jesus (Rev. 19:10); the angel repeats his prohibition at the end of the work in slightly different words (Rev. 22:9). Thus, even as he remains on earth, John is not only a member of the kingdom of priests but has also become like the angels. But perhaps most remarkable, the angel attributes angelic status not only to the visionary but to all true followers of Christ, living or dead.

The Righteous Dead in the Ascension of Isaiah

The Ascension of Isaiah is a composite work that consists of a narrative of Isaiah's martyrdom at the hands of the wicked king Manasseh (Asc. Isa. 1–5) and an account of Isaiah's ascent to heaven sometime before the martyrdom (Asc. Isa. 6–11). The complete work is preserved only in Ethiopic, but the ascent is preserved in Slavonic and Latin as well; there are Greek and Latin fragments of the martyrdom and Coptic fragments of both sections. The Ascension in its current form is a Christian work with Christian concerns central to both sections, although some scholars believe that the martyrdom was an originally Jewish composition. The contents of the ascent, and particularly its understanding of Christ as an exalted angel, fit well in the early second century.

The ascent takes place as the prophet Isaiah speaks before Hezekiah, the pious king of Judah who was the father of Manasseh, his courtiers, and the prophet's disciples. As Isaiah speaks, the voice of the Holy Spirit is heard, Isaiah falls silent, and his spirit ascends to heaven though his body remains behind (Asc. Isa. 6). The culmination of the ascent is Isaiah's vision of the descent of Christ from the seventh heaven to earth, his incarnation, life, and crucifixion, and finally his triumphant ascent (Asc. Isa. 10–11).

But for our purposes it is the ascent itself, and particularly Isaiah's experience among the angels and the righteous dead in the seventh heaven, that are of most interest.

As Isaiah and his angelic guide pass through each of the first five heavens, they see an angel seated on a throne with angels on the right and left; the angels on the right are superior to the angels on the left, and the angel on the throne is more glorious than the others. All the angels sing praises to God and his Beloved, who are enthroned in the seventh heaven, but the praise of the angels on the right is superior to the praise of the angels on the left. Each succeeding heaven is more glorious than the one before, and as he ascends, Isaiah undergoes a physical transformation: "My face was becoming brighter and brighter as I went up from heaven to heaven" (Asc. Isa. 7:25).

The sixth heaven marks a new stage of holiness and glory. In the sixth heaven, when Isaiah addresses his angelic guide as "lord," the angel responds, "I am not your lord but your companion" (Asc. Isa. 8:5), just as the angel tells John in the book of Revelation; indeed, according to the angel, no living man has ever seen what Isaiah has seen (Asc. Isa. 8:11). The sixth and seventh heavens are distinguished from the lower heavens by the equality that exists among their angels: there is no throne in the middle, and the angels on the left are equal to the angels on the right. The angelic guide promises Isaiah that when he leaves his body permanently he will be given a garment and will become the equal of the angels of the seventh heaven (Asc. Isa. 8:14–15). When Isaiah and his guide join the praises in the sixth heaven, "our praises were like theirs" (Asc. Isa. 8:17). Once again, participation in the angelic liturgy is a way of manifesting angelic status.

The seventh heaven is even more glorious than the sixth. As he tries to enter the heaven, a voice challenges Isaiah (Asc. Isa. 9:1). But as Isaiah trembles in fear, Christ himself permits his entrance (Asc. Isa. 9:2–5). In the seventh heaven Isaiah finds the righteous dead, "stripped of the garments of the flesh … in their garments of the world above, and they were like angels, standing there in great glory" (Asc. Isa. 9:7, 9). Yet it emerges that the ultimate fate of the righteous will be even more glorious. After Christ has "plundered the angel of death" and brought the remaining righteous dead to heaven, the righteous will receive thrones and crowns of glory in addition to their garments (Asc. Isa. 9:10–18).

In the seventh heaven Isaiah also sees a book in which are recorded all the deeds of the children of Israel as well as the deeds of others whom Isaiah does not know, presumably gentiles who become Christians (Asc. Isa. 9:21–2), and the garments, thrones, and crowns stored up for these future righteous (Asc. Isa. 9:24–6). The book recalls the books opened before the Ancient of Days in Daniel 7; it is the collective counterpart to the scrolls recording the visionary's deeds in the Apocalypse of Zephaniah. The heaven of the Ascension of Isaiah thus combines elements of royal court and temple, reflected in the presence of the book in the seventh heaven and the liturgical activity of each heaven, respectively.

In the sixth heaven, Isaiah's praise was equal to that of the angels. In the seventh heaven Isaiah is able to join the righteous dead in worshiping Christ and the Holy Spirit (Asc. Isa. 9:27–36), while the angels offer their praise only after the righteous. So too in the worship of God himself, the righteous follow Christ and the Holy Spirit in offering praise, while the angels follow the righteous. Furthermore, the righteous are able to look upon God with a steady gaze while the angels are not. Isaiah is able to glance at God momentarily, but not to maintain his gaze. Thus, after the equality of the sixth heaven, hierarchy has reemerged in the seventh heaven, and hierarchy of a somewhat surprising kind: the righteous dead clearly stand above the angels, while Isaiah occupies a spot between them.

Angels, the Living, and the Dead

From one point of view, the claim that human beings who have jettisoned their earthly bodies can become like the angels is less surprising than the claim that Enoch, Abraham, and Isaiah could become like the angels while still alive. Still, both claims insist on the continuity between humanity and the divine, and the picture of the righteous dead as the equals of the angels is more radical in the sense that it is more inclusive. Yet there are significant differences among the apocalypses on the extent of that equality. The Parables of Enoch and the book of Revelation simply do not address the question; they show the righteous dead participating in the divine liturgy but offer no clues about their status relative to the angels. In the Apocalypse of Zephaniah, as we saw, only the most exalted of the righteous dead are on the level of the highest angels. The garments put on by more ordinary righteous souls make them like lower orders of angels; they still cannot approach the highest angels. In the Ascension of Isaiah, on the other hand, the righteous dead as a group enjoy a status higher than that of the angels. The understanding of the righteous dead as exalted above the angels makes sense for a small sectarian group that sees itself in opposition to the outside world and that understands righteousness to be impossible apart from membership in the group; such a self-understanding would not be surprising for a group of second-century Christians. A sectarian worldview may also explain the willingness of the book of Revelation to extend angelic status even to living followers of Christ. The Apocalypse of Zephaniah, on the other hand, appears to come from a community with a less sectarian view of the world. Not all of its members are saints of the highest caliber. Its hero committed sins in his life and, unlike the great biblical heroes, he is not the equal of the highest angels, yet he is granted a place in paradise nonetheless.

Cosmological Wonders in the Parables and 2 Enoch

Sacred geography and the wonders of nature are an important part of the sights Enoch sees in the course of his journey to the ends of the earth in the Book of the Watchers. Since later ascent apocalypses are concerned only with the heavens, they have no room for geography or even for some of the natural wonders of Enoch's journey, such as spice trees, beasts, and birds. The gates through which the stars, the winds, snow, rain, and dew and other meteorological phenomena emerge, on the other hand, are more promising material for the later ascent apocalypses; these phenomena originate in the heavens and might well be seen by a visionary ascending through the heavens. Yet only three of the later ascent apocalypses, the Parables of Enoch, 2 Enoch, and

3 Baruch, take up these themes, and the first two are particularly closely linked to the Book of the Watchers.

The ancient Israelite Wisdom tradition expressed in the psalms and the book of Proverbs claimed that nature, and the heavens specifically, publicly testify to their creator: "The heavens are telling the glory of God; and the firmament proclaims his handiwork" (Ps. 19:1). In the book of Job, in contrast, God silences Job by describing the marvels of creation (Job 38–42): they may testify to their creator, but they also testify to the human inability to comprehend him. The Book of the Watchers takes a middle course. The wonders of nature demand that we praise God, yet only Enoch, an extraordinarily righteous hero who travels to the ends of the earth in the company of the angels, has seen them. Still, the rest of us can learn of those wonders through Enoch's account of his journey.

The loss of interest in natural phenomena, even heavenly ones, in the ascent apocalypses that follow the Book of the Watchers may reflect growing pessimism about the value of the created world. Such an attitude certainly lies behind the reworking of themes from the Book of the Watchers in the Parables (1 Enoch 41–4, 59–60). On the one hand, the Parables values heavenly natural phenomena that allude to the piety of the righteous:

> And I saw other lightnings and stars of heaven; and I saw that he called them by their names, and they listened to him. And I saw a righteous balance, how they are weighed according to their light, according to the breadth of their spaces and the day of their appearing. (And I saw how) their motion produces lightning, and their motion is according to the number of the angels, and they keep their faith with one another. And I asked the angel who went with me and showed me what was hidden, "What are these?" And he said to me, "The Lord of Spirits has shown you a parable concerning them; these are the names of the holy ones who dwell on the earth and believe in the name of the Lord of Spirits forever and ever." (1 Enoch 43:1–4)

This comparison of the faithfulness of the righteous to the faithfulness of nature, which helps to explain the work's self-designation as "parables," owes less to the journey to the ends of the earth than to the opening chapters of the Book of the Watchers (1 Enoch 2–5), which contrast the faithfulness of nature to the faithlessness of humanity, though the Parables instead focuses on the minority of humanity that behaves like nature. The Parables shares Job's view that Wisdom is unavailable to human beings: "Wisdom went forth to dwell among the sons of men, but she did not find a dwelling. Wisdom returned to her place, and sat down among the angels" (1 Enoch 42:2). In light of this view, it is not surprising that natural phenomena are understood as "secrets" (1 Enoch 41:1, 59:1–3). Thus the Parables' sense that the times are out of joint leads it to doubt that earthly natural phenomena can offer any testimony to the creator. Even the wonders of the heavens do not proclaim God's glory, as the psalm would have it, but rather whisper their secrets.

Natural phenomena similar to those noted in the Parables appear in the first heaven of 2 Enoch: stars and constellations, the heavenly sea, and meteorological phenomena, together with their angelic supervisors. In the fourth heaven Enoch sees the paths of the sun and moon and the doors through which they travel; the relatively brief description of the paths and their calendrical implications recalls the much more elaborate account in the Astronomical Book. Some scholars have seen the 364-day calendar 2 Enoch embraces as reflecting later Christian calendrical concerns. In contrast to the Astronomical Book, the account in 2 Enoch contains elements of personification of the sun and moon. Both heavenly luminaries travel on chariots drawn by many-winged angels (2 Enoch 6), and the sun wears a crown when it shines on the earth. In the tour to the ends of the earth in the Book of the Watchers Enoch praised God in response to the sights he saw. In 2 Enoch, it is not the sights Enoch sees that elicit praise but the sounds of the angelic liturgy. On the other hand, there is no evidence in 2 Enoch of the extremely negative view of life on earth that permeates the Parables' picture of natural phenomena.

Yet God's role as creator of the world is clearly of crucial importance to 2 Enoch. It is the subject of the revelation Enoch receives upon arrival in the seventh heaven, and the work marks it as of particular significance: "Not even to my angels have I revealed my secret ... nor do they know how my infinite and incomprehensible creation was accomplished; yet I am revealing it to you today" (2 Enoch 11:3). 2 Enoch's account of creation plays on the Genesis account but introduces two mysterious figures that God summons from the abyss at the very beginning of the process of creation. Adoil is "immense in size" with "a great age in his belly"; light emerges from him and is established as the foundation of things above. Aruchaz is "hard, heavy, and very black," and he becomes the foundation of things below. Much about this narrative is unclear, but its underlying purpose seems to be to improve on the biblical creation account's picture of direct contact between God and the world. For some ancient Jews and Christians, this picture was deeply troubling because it required the exalted and spiritual God to entangle himself with the material world. The idea of emanation that developed in Platonic circles in the early centuries of this era addresses the same problem through the image of the sun: just as the sun sends out rays of light that illumine the world without in anyway being diminished, so the godhead unfolds itself to reach and order the material, leaving the godhead itself free of the taint of materiality. The figures of Adoil and Aruchaz are a far more concrete way of expressing this idea, but they too serve as intermediaries who distance God from contact with the material world.

3 Baruch

Like 4 Ezra and 2 Baruch, 3 Baruch opens with its hero mourning the destruction of the Temple. 4 Ezra and 2 Baruch go on to question and ultimately defend God's justice through visions of the Last Judgment and the messianic age. 3 Baruch addresses the same problem through an ascent to heaven to see sights the angelic guide characterizes as "mysteries." These "mysteries" consist of the post-mortem reward and punishment of souls, the tree of life from the Garden of Eden, the courses of the sun and moon, and the heavenly temple. All are sights familiar from other ascent apocalypses, but the treatment of these themes in 3 Baruch is distinctive.

3 Baruch survives in two versions, Greek and Slavonic, that contain significant differences. The original language of the work was Greek, but the Slavonic appears to preserve an earlier form of the work than the Greek that has come down to us. Both versions contain Christian elements, but the Christian elements of the Greek go beyond those of the Slavonic. Most scholars take this difference as evidence for an originally Jewish version of 3 Baruch that was gradually Christianized. This scenario is certainly plausible, but the lack of interest in the earthly Temple, Jerusalem, or the people of Israel, suggests to me that even the earliest form of 3 Baruch was a Christian composition. Further study of the Slavonic version may advance the discussion.

The distance between 3 Baruch and the works that must have served as its models is evident from the first heaven on. In the first heaven Baruch finds the builders of the Tower of Babel who have been given the faces and feet of animals in punishment for their efforts. The second heaven is occupied by the planners of the Tower undergoing a similar punishment. The story of the Tower of Babel does not figure in any other apocalypse, and 3 Baruch offers no explanation of the relevance of the story for its concerns. But a clue to its appeal may be found in the third heaven, where Baruch sees, among other sights, a vine that is identified as the tree from which Adam and Eve ate in the Garden of Eden. This allusion to the most important biblical explanation for the origins of evil, which puts the blame squarely on humanity, suggests that 3 Baruch was uncomfortable with the picture of the story of the watchers, in which angelic misdeeds are the cause of evil in the world. The story of the Tower of Babel, the concluding episode in the primeval history that begins with creation and the story of the Garden of Eden, shows that even the Flood did not bring an end to human sin and rebellion. By substituting the punishment of the human builders and planners of the Tower for the punishment of the watchers, 3 Baruch leaves no doubt that humanity is to blame for the mess in which it finds itself.

In the third heaven Baruch also sees the paths of the sun and moon. The personification implicit in 2 Enoch is explicit in 3 Baruch: the sun is a man, and he wears a crown of fire (3 Baruch 6:2), while the moon is a woman (3 Baruch 9:3). Unlike 2 Enoch,

3 Baruch shows no interest in the calendrical implications of the paths of sun and moon. Like the Parables it uses nature to criticize the sins of humanity, though it does so quite differently. While the Parables contrasts the faithfulness of nature with the faithlessness of humanity, 3 Baruch describes the deleterious affects of the sins of humanity on the sun: his crown requires cleaning each night because of the sins he has seen (3 Baruch 8:5). But 3 Baruch is concerned not only with how the sun reminds us of human depravity but also with how his mode of travel through the heavens attests God's greatness. According to 3 Baruch the sun is accompanied in his travels by a phoenix. This extraordinary bird flies in front of the sun to protect the earth from the sun's rays (3 Baruch 6:1–10); it eats manna (3 Baruch 6:11), and, according to the Greek, cinnamon is its excrement (3 Baruch 6:12). By the end of each day the bird is exhausted because of the fiery rays it has had to absorb (3 Baruch 8:5–6), but without the phoenix no living creature could survive the sun's heat (3 Baruch, both versions: Slavonic, 6:6; Greek, 8:7). In the Book of the Watchers Enoch responds to the wonders of nature by praising God. In 2 Enoch, Enoch praises God in response to the angelic praise already taking place in the fourth heaven where sun and moon are found. Baruch, in contrast, is generally impassive in response to the sights he is shown. The only exception is the sight of the sun and the phoenix. Upon seeing them, Baruch is overcome by fear at their "glory" and hides in the wings of his angelic guide (3 Baruch: Slavonic, 8:6; Greek, 7:5).

Baruch's ascent takes him only as far as the fifth heaven, but since the archangel Michael must ascend still further to see God, there is clearly at least one more heaven above and more likely two, since a six-heaven schema is nowhere else attested. Furthermore, there are some indications that 3 Baruch as it has come down to us is an abridgment of an earlier form of the work that allowed Baruch to ascend to the highest heaven and see more of the workings of the heavenly temple than he sees in the extant version.

In all of the other ascent apocalypses discussed, the visionaries, including the dead soul of the Apocalypse of Zephaniah, achieve angelic status. Baruch does not. It is not impossible that the original form of the work showed him gaining equality with his angelic guide upon their arrival in the sixth heaven as Isaiah does in the Ascension of Isaiah, but in light of Baruch's reaction to the phoenix this seems unlikely. Rather, like 4 Ezra, 3 Baruch appears to be an apocalypse that offers a critique of other apocalypses. It insists that the gap between humanity and the divine is irreducible, even for those who ascend to heaven, just as it insists, against the Enochic tradition, that responsibility for the sad state of affairs on earth rests firmly with humanity.

Chapter 6

Tours of Paradise and Hell
and the Hekhalot Texts

In the centuries following the composition of the ascent apocalypses treated in the last chapter, Jews and Christians continued to compose works in which the visionary traveled to heaven or places otherwise inaccessible to ordinary human beings. One important corpus of such works consists of tours of paradise and hell, or, often, hell alone, which were extremely popular among Christians in late antiquity and the Middle Ages. Another such corpus is the hekhalot texts, Jewish mystical works that include descriptions of ascent through the seven palaces to behold God seated on his chariot-throne and instruction for such ascents.

Tours of Paradise and Hell

If the founding text in the tradition of ascent apocalypses is the ascent to heaven in the Book of the Watchers, the ultimate ancestor of the tours of paradise and hell is Enoch's journey to the ends of the earth. There is, to be sure, considerable distance between the Book of the Watchers' brief description of the chambers in which the souls of the dead await the eschaton and the elaborate descriptions of hell and paradise in the later apocalypses. The tours of hell and paradise are also more focused in their interests than the journey to the ends of the earth, during which Enoch sees a variety of sights including important locations of mythic geography, natural wonders, and cosmological phenomena. But the presence in the later tours of the same kind of demonstrative explanations found in the journey to the ends of the earth in the Book of the Watchers attests to their debt.

The Apocalypse of Peter

The Apocalypse of Peter, the earliest surviving apocalypse to focus on paradise and hell, was probably composed in the second century CE, roughly contemporary with the latest of the ascent apocalypses considered in the previous chapter. Unlike the Apocalypse of Paul and the apocalypses that draw on it, the original form of the Apocalypse of Peter does not involve a tour. Rather, the description of hell appears in the course of a prophecy by Jesus to his disciples about the last days and the great judgment. The punishments of hell await the wicked at the Second Coming. So too the righteous will enjoy paradise, mentioned very briefly, only in the future. The work concludes with a retelling of the episode of the transfiguration from the synoptic gospels. This form of the Apocalypse of Peter is preserved in Ethiopic, a translation, perhaps indirect, of the original Greek.

The most extensive Greek text of the Apocalypse of Peter to reach us is the Akhmim fragment, which dates to the eighth or ninth century CE and was found in the same grave as a Greek text of most of the Book of the Watchers. While its description of the contents of hell is quite close to that of the Ethiopic, its picture of paradise is more elaborate, taking over material that in the Ethiopic version forms part of the transfiguration narrative. But the Akhmim Greek turns the prophecy of the Ethiopic version into a tour. The redactor responsible for this change must have shared the belief dominant among Jews and Christians from the early centuries of this era that souls receive their reward or punishment immediately after death. The Ethiopic version's picture of reward and punishment in the future shows that the original form of the Apocalypse of Peter shared the view of earlier works such as the Book of the Watchers and Daniel that reward and punishment await the Last Judgment.

The sins for which the wicked are punished in the Apocalypse of Peter include blasphemy, murder, betrayal, usury, and a variety of sexual sins, including fornication, homosexuality, and abortion. The prominence of sexual sins and sins of speech in the Apocalypse of Peter and later tours of hell is presumably related to the fact that these sins are largely invisible: murder and theft are sins that almost inevitably come to light, but a community is likely to be unaware of sexual or verbal sins that take place in its midst.

Beyond their horror, the most striking characteristic of the punishments in the Apocalypse of Peter is that so many of them are designed to respond to the particular sins of the wrongdoers to whom they are assigned. Thus, for example, those whose lies led to the deaths of the martyrs have their lips cut off while fire burns their mouths and insides, and those who trusted in riches and persecuted widows and orphans are dressed in filthy rags as they are cast upon a sharp pillar of fire (Apoc. Pet. 9). Usually the sin for which the sinners are being punished is identified with a demonstrative explanation: "These are they who lent money and took usury" (Apoc. Pet. 10). Demonstrative explanations, which constitute a further link to the Book of the Watchers, this one of form rather than content, appear in virtually all the tours of hell that follow the Apocalypse of Peter. They also appear in descriptions of hell related to those in the Christian tours that are found in rabbinic and medieval Jewish texts; some of these descriptions are clearly fragments of earlier works.

One distinctive group of punishments in the Apocalypse of Peter involves hanging by the sinful limb: blasphemers hang in fire by their tongues, fornicating women are hung by their hair, presumably in punishment for immodesty, and their male partners hang by their thighs (Apoc. Pet. 7). These punishments are of particular interest because they also appear in the Jewish traditions about hell just noted. A few of the later Christian tours of hell also contain hanging punishments, but these punishments are not as close to those in the Apocalypse of Peter as are the hanging punishments of the Jewish texts. Eventually hanging punishments disappear altogether from Christian tours of hell.

The presence in later Jewish texts of a group of punishments known from the earliest Christian vision of hell but not from later Christian works suggests that the Apocalypse of Peter drew on an early Jewish source or sources, perhaps a vision or tour of hell attributed to Elijah and Isaiah, who figure in the later Jewish traditions about hell. Such a work might have included in its tour other topics of interest to the ascent apocalypses discussed in the last chapter. It could have placed hell and paradise in one of the heavens as 2 Enoch does, or offered a vision of future reward and punishment after an ascent as the Slavonic version of 3 Baruch appears to do. The work surely contained demonstrative explanations, which appear even in the very fragmentary passages preserved in later Jewish works.

The Apocalypse of Paul

In the centuries that followed the composition of the Apocalypse of Peter, tours of paradise and hell became a favorite genre for Christian writers. The most influential of these tours was the Apocalypse of Paul. Though clearly indebted to the Apocalypse of Peter, the Apocalypse of Paul differs from it in important ways. As already noted, unlike the original version of the Apocalypse of Peter, it understands reward and punishment to take place immediately after death rather than at the Last Judgment and can thus present its vision of paradise and hell as a tour. Its picture of hell shares aspects of the picture in the Apocalypse of Peter, but the emphases are somewhat different, and while the Apocalypse of Peter promotes righteous behavior primarily by warning about the punishments for unrighteous behavior, the Apocalypse of Paul also devotes considerable time to the rewards of the righteous.

Recent scholarship locates the composition of the Apocalypse of Paul in the late fourth or early fifth century. Its prologue describes the miraculous discovery of the work in a marble box hidden in the foundations of the house in Tarsus in which Paul had lived; it dates the discovery to the year 388. If, as recent scholarship has argued, the prologue is original, the Apocalypse of Paul could not have been put into circulation any earlier than the date the prologue provides. The work's embrace of asceticism, the high value placed on virginity, and the prominence of the sins of pride and hypocrisy, are all characteristic of a monastic setting, and by the end of the fourth century monastic communities were well established in Egypt, where the Apocalypse of Paul was probably written. The original language of the Apocalypse of Paul was Greek, but while the Greek survives only in much-abbreviated form, the Latin appears to be a translation of the full Greek text. Because the Latin text forms the basis for most modern translations, the work is often known as the Vision of Paul after the Latin title, *Visio Pauli*.

The Apocalypse of Paul takes as its point of departure the famous passage in 2 Corinthians where Paul claims to have ascended to paradise in the third heaven and heard "unutterable words that it is not lawful for one to speak" (2 Cor. 12:2–4; my trans.). The reference to the passage in 2 Corinthians is followed by the prologue describing the discovery of the work (Apoc. Paul 1–2) and God's commissioning of Paul to rebuke his people for their misdeeds (Apoc. Paul 3–10). Then Paul is taken up to the third heaven (Apoc. Paul 11–18), where he is shown souls departing from the body at the moment of death. The righteous soul is greeted by a group of joyful angels who take him before God for judgment. The wicked soul, on the other hand, is turned over to evil angels in a scene that recalls the vision of the terrifying angels who come to accompany the souls of the wicked at death in the Apocalypse of Zephaniah. As we will see shortly, there is other evidence that the Apocalypse of Paul made use of the Apocalypse of Zephaniah.

Now Paul makes a brief visit to paradise, located in the third heaven as 2 Corinthians requires, where he is greeted by the two heroes of the Hebrew Bible who never died, Enoch and Elijah (Apoc. Paul 19–20); in keeping with 2 Corinthians, Paul is unable to reveal to humanity what he saw and heard there. His angelic guide then takes him from the third heaven back to earth, where he sees the land of promise, where the righteous will dwell during the millennium, enjoying its marvelous fertility (Apoc. Paul 21–2).

Next, in a scene clearly indebted to the Apocalypse of Zephaniah, Paul traverses Lake Acherusia in a golden boat to arrive at the city of Christ (Apoc. Paul 23). As we saw in the previous chapter, the scene from the Apocalypse of Zephaniah comes at the end of a series of ordeals the visionary undergoes. After having proved his worth, the visionary is placed in a boat and given an angelic garment that allows him to understand the language of the angels;

unlike the visionaries of other ascent apocalypses, however, he never achieves the status of the highest angels. Yet though the author of the Apocalypse of Paul surely understood his hero to outrank the hero of the Apocalypse of Zephaniah, who is not a great hero of the past but an ordinary righteous soul, he makes no mention of an angelic garment or of Paul's ability to understand angelic language. For the Apocalypse of Paul, it appears, the boundary separating humanity from angels is no longer permeable, not even for a great hero like Paul.

Arriving in the city of Christ, Paul meets the righteous dead, including the patriarchs and prophets, and tours the city (Apoc. Paul 23–30). Four rivers, of honey, milk, wine, and oil, go forth from the city; there are golden thrones at its gates, and an altar at which David sings at its center. Just outside the city, unable to enter, are men who lived as pious ascetics but were guilty of the sin of pride.

From the city of Christ Paul goes on to visit the place of punishment (Apoc. Paul 31–42). The dominant form of punishment in the Apocalypse of Paul is fire, including fiery rivers and pits, and there are more worms, beasts, and tormenting angels than in the Apocalypse of Peter. The Apocalypse of Paul also develops its own form of measure-for-measure punishment in which sinners stand up to the offending body part in a fiery river. As in the Apocalypse of Peter, male and female adulterers are punished by hanging, though the male adulterers hang not by their thighs but by their eyebrows. The Apocalypse of Paul does not contain a hanging punishment for blasphemy. It is possible that the similarities of the Apocalypse of Paul to the Apocalypse of Peter are to be explained by direct dependence. But the evidence of the Jewish fragments suggests that the Apocalypse of Peter was not the only possible source for measure-for-measure hanging punishments, and the significant differences not only in the overall pictures of hell but in the details of the sins and the punishments they share make it likely that the Apocalypse of Paul did not draw directly on the Apocalypse of Peter but on descriptions of hell indebted to it or to its sources.

The Apocalypse of Paul's hell contains many more groups of sinners than the hell of the Apocalypse of Peter. Sexual sins and sins of speech continue to play a significant role, presumably for

the reasons suggested above, but the Apocalypse of Paul introduces a new type of sinner, the church official. In his tour Paul
sees four types of official – a presbyter, a bishop, a deacon, and a
lector – undergoing punishment for failing to live up their offices.
The presence of these officials in hell reflects the institutionaliza-
tion of the church that had occurred by the time the Apocalypse
of Paul was written, and perhaps also a monastic author's skepti-
cism about the piety of non-monastic clergy.

After having seen the horrors of hell Paul begins to weep, and
soon he is joined by the sinners, who beg for mercy, and the archangel Michael and his angels (Apoc. Paul 43). In answer to their
prayers the Son of God appears and promises Sunday rest to the
wicked in hell (Apoc. Paul 44). With this achievement, Paul
returns to paradise (Apoc. Paul 45–51), where the apocalypse
concludes: the Virgin Mary, the patriarchs, Moses, the prophets,
John the Baptist, and Adam all come to meet Paul and greet him
graciously. By now any reader would surely have concluded that,
even with Sunday off, sin does not pay.

Descendants of the Apocalypse of Paul

The Apocalypse of Paul was an extremely popular work in late
antiquity and the Middle Ages. It was translated into Syriac,
Coptic, Armenian, and Slavonic, and in the centuries following
its composition up until perhaps the twelfth century it gave rise
to many imitators: in Ethiopic, the Apocalypse of Mary, the
Apocalypse of Baruch, and the Apocalypse of Gorgorios; in Greek,
the Apocalypse of Mary and the Apocalypse of Ezra; and in Latin,
the Vision of Ezra and eight different redactions of the Latin version of the Apocalypse of Paul, which were then translated into
vernacular languages across Europe. It is not surprising that this
extensive textual tradition also left its mark on visions attributed
to contemporary figures in medieval chronicles. The most famous
work to show the influence of this tradition is Dante's *Divine
Comedy*, which reveals knowledge of a form of the Apocalypse of
Paul. The tours of paradise and hell also had an impact on Muslim
literature, particularly on accounts of the *isra'*, Mohammed's
night journey from Mecca to Jerusalem, to which there is a brief

and enigmatic allusion in Sura 17 of the Qur'an, and the *mi'rāj*, Mohammed's ascent to heaven, which is also derived from Sura 17.

But later authors and redactors did not find all parts of the Apocalypse of Paul equally interesting. Thus, while the three Ethiopic works listed above treat most of the subjects that appear in the Apocalypse of Paul, the rest of the works mentioned are devoted almost exclusively to the tour of hell, sometimes virtually free-standing, in other cases placed within a new frame; paradise is mentioned but not explored in some of these works, while in others it is entirely absent. It is not hard to understand the reasons why hell was of more interest to both authors and audiences than paradise. From the authors' point of view, it was probably a reasonable assessment of human nature to conclude that fear of punishment is more effective in deterring sin than promise of reward is in promoting goodness. Authors may also have found greater scope for their imagination in refining old punishments and developing new ones than in improving on paradise, a place of such perfection as to be of necessity rather boring. And the obvious popularity of works focusing on hell alone suggests that medieval audiences shared the not very admirable but entirely human ability to take pleasure in the misfortunes of others. Hell turned out to be more entertaining than paradise.

Hekhalot Texts

The hekhalot literature consists of five compositions written in Hebrew in the post-rabbinic period, starting perhaps in the seventh century, together with a number of shorter passages transmitted in manuscripts with them; in addition, the Cairo Genizah provides evidence of hekhalot works that have been lost as well as of alternate versions of some of the surviving texts. The corpus take its name from the term *hekhalot* (sing. *hekhal*), temples or palaces, which these texts use to refer to the seven levels through which the visionary passes. Where God is concerned, as we have already seen in the apocalypses, temple and palace are two sides of the same coin: since a temple is a house of God, a palace in which God dwells is by definition a temple. In some of the hekhalot texts, the visionary's journey is referred to as descent rather than ascent. Scholars have offered a variety of explanation for this rather surprising terminology, but as yet no consensus has emerged.

Like the apocalypses, the hekhalot texts are pseudepigraphic compositions, but unlike the apocalypses, which take as their heroes great figures of the biblical past, the hekhalot texts choose great rabbis, particularly Rabbi Aqiba and Rabbi Ishmael, two of the most important figures of the early second century CE. *Sefer Hekhalot*, the Book of Hekhalot, also known as 3 Enoch, constitutes a partial exception to this generalization; its protagonist is R. Ishmael, but much of what he reports concerns the career of the great hero of apocalyptic literature, Enoch. I will have more to say below about this work, which is unusual among the hekhalot texts in other ways as well.

The contents of the hekhalot texts include descriptions of the seven hekhalot, the angels who inhabit them, the divine throne, and the liturgy performed before it; the words of the hymns that form the liturgy; angelic and divine names; rituals designed to summon angels for purposes ranging from help in Torah study to the attainment of wealth and success; and a fairly small number of passages prescribing rituals designed to produce ascent (or descent) to the chariot. Not all of the individual works contain all of these elements. The texts are composed of units of varying size that may once have circulated independently of their current context. The content of individual works can vary considerably from manuscript to manuscript, and the boundaries of the works are sometimes blurry. The shape and arrangement of the units is quite loose, though some give evidence of an editorial hand that exercised considerable selectivity.

As my brief description of their content suggests, the hekhalot texts share a number of interests with the ascent apocalypses – ascent itself, the angels and their liturgy, the divine throne – but the range of their interests and their form are significantly different from those of the apocalypses. Only in the case of *Sefer Hekhalot* (3 Enoch) are there any grounds for suggesting a literary connection. I shall return to the problem of the relationship between the two bodies of literature after I have discussed the themes of the hekhalot texts most relevant for our purposes.

Ascent through the Seven Hekhalot

Though there are many references to ascent in the hekhalot texts, there are rather few descriptions of the process. Outside of *Sefer Hekhalot* (3 Enoch), which will be discussed at the end of this chapter, the only narrative of ascent of any length in hekhalot literature appears in *Hekhalot Rabbati*, Greater Hekhalot, which refers to the process as descent. In the passage in question, R. Ishmael reports on R. Nehuniah ben haQanah's revelation of instructions for descent to the chariot-throne to the rabbis assembled in the Temple precincts as R. Nehuniah stands before the divine throne in the seventh hekhal. The story provides some detail about the technique R. Ishmael uses to recall R. Nehuniah from before the throne to answer the assembled rabbis' question about a crucial but enigmatic phrase in his instructions about a danger at the sixth hekhal (*HR* 224–8), but it tells us nothing about how R. Nehuniah accomplished his descent in the first place. The instructions for descent are clearly composed from two separate sources, which follow one on the other (*HR* 204–18, 219–37). Yet each set contains something the other set lacks, so it is possible that their juxtaposition was intended to create a single set of comprehensive instructions.

The first set of instructions begins with directions on how to set the descent in motion:

> When a man wishes to descend to the chariot, he should call upon Surya the Prince of the Presence and adjure him 112 times in the name of Totrosyay YHWH, who is called Totrosyay Zurtaq Totraviel ... [there follow several more names, twelve in all in most of the manuscripts] YHWH God of Israel. He should not add to the 112 times nor should he subtract from them, and if he adds or subtracts, he is responsible for any harm that befalls him. Let his mouth bring forth the names, and let the fingers of his hands count 112. Immediately he will descend and rule over the chariot. (*HR* 204–5)

For each hekhal the instructions provide a list of the names of the eight angels who guard its entrance, four on each side, and a more extended description of the terrifying guardians of the seventh hekhal and their marvelous horses. This section concludes with the visionary standing unharmed in the seventh hekhal, joining in the angelic liturgy before the divine throne.

The second set of instructions lacks information about how to set the descent in motion. Instead it begins with the visionary at the entrance to the first hekhal:

> Rabbi Ishmael said, When you come and stand at the gate of the first hekhal, take two seals in your two hands, one of Totrosyay YHWH and one of Surya the Prince of the Presence. Show the seal of Totrosyay YHWH to those who stand on the right and the seal of Surya to those who stand on the left. Immediately Dahaviel the Prince, the chief of the gate of the first palace who is in charge of the first hekhal and stands on the right of the threshold, and Tufahiel the Prince, who stands with him on the left of the threshold, take hold of you, one your left hand, the other your right hand, and lead you and hand you over to Tagriel the Prince, chief of the gate of the second hekhal, who stands on the right of the threshold, and Matpiel the Prince, who stands with him on the left of the threshold, and finish by cautioning you ... (HR 219)

The visionary is to follow this procedure at the gate to each successive hekhal.

There are two conclusions to this portion of the instructions. They have not been thoroughly integrated, but both understand the goal of the journey through the hekhalot as participation in the angelic liturgy. In the first conclusion, the visionary takes his place among the angelic host that stands before the chariot-throne. In the second, he begins to sing the song with which the throne itself addresses God. The understanding of participation in the angelic liturgy as the culmination of ascent recalls the Apocalypse of Zephaniah, in which the visionary joins in the angelic songs of praise after donning an angelic garment. The song of the throne recalls the Apocalypse of Abraham, in which Abraham discovers on his arrival in heaven that the song his angelic guide taught him to keep him safe during his ascent is the song sung by the creatures that support the throne.

Hekhalot Zutarti, Lesser Hekhalot, contains a set of instructions quite similar to the second set in *Hekhalot Rabbati*:

> Over the first hekhal is appointed Tetrosay YHWH the Prince, a proud prince who exalts his king. Therefore he is appointed over the first hekhal. You show him the seal and ring on which is engraved Nehafdariel Lord God of Israel, our father who is in heaven. (*HZ* 416)

After describing the procedure for entering the first hekhal, most of the manuscripts skip to the sixth hekhal; it appears that that the intervening material, preserved in one of the manuscripts, has fallen out. Indeed, most of the manuscripts refer to the sixth hekhal rather than the first in the sentence beginning "Therefore"; this identification is presumably a change intended to bring sense to the passage after the instructions for the second through fifth hekhalot had fallen out. Even without the loss of the intermediate hekhalot the instructions in *Hekhalot Zutarti* are quite streamlined compared to those of *Hekhalot Rabbati*. Like the second set of instructions in *Hekhalot Rabbati*, the instructions in *Hekhalot Zutarti* provide no information about how to undertake the ascent but assume that the ascent is already in progress. Since in *Hekhalot Zutarti* a single angel guards the gates of each hekhal, the visionary needs only a single seal in order to enter. Furthermore, there is no description of how the visionary is handed on from angel to angel. But *Hekhalot Zutarti* does provide one detail lacking in *Hekhalot Rabbati*: the seal to be shown to the angelic gatekeeper is engraved on a ring. As in *Hekhalot Rabbati*, the names of the angelic guards and the divine names on the seals are multisyllabic and usually without any clear meaning; in both works, not surprisingly, they vary from manuscript to manuscript.

But despite the similarity of their pictures of the hekhalot and the process of descent or ascent, the goal of the journey in the two sets of instructions is very different. In *Hekhalot Zutarti*, after the visionary has successfully entered the seventh hekhal, he is passed from angel to angel until he finds himself sitting in God's lap. There the visionary is to ask God to make his servants, that is, the angels, do whatever the visionary desires; the text provides the words to be used in making this request. The visionary's ascent thus allows him to avoid the trouble of adjuring individual angels himself, a practice of considerable importance in the hekhalot texts. Yet despite – or perhaps because of – the self-serving character of his request, the visionary is instructed to address God as his beloved in language drawn from Song of Songs (*HZ* 417–19).

The picture of angelic guardians at the gates of each heaven does not play much of a role in the ascent apocalypses, but it does appear in the portion of the Ascension of Isaiah that describes Christ's descent to earth. Once he reaches the lowest heavens, Christ must give a password to the angelic gatekeepers (Asc. Isa. 10:23–31). But the picture must have been more widespread in the early centuries of this era. Celsus, the second-century critic of Christianity, apparently claimed that Christians learned the names of the heavenly doorkeepers to facilitate their passage through the heavens, for in his refutation of Celsus' work, the third-century Church Father Origen insists it was not true Christians but the Ophites, a Gnostic sect, who engaged in this practice (*Against Celsus* 7.40).

Danger and Testing

From Enoch in the Book of the Watchers on, the heroes of the apocalypses show fear as they ascend through the heavens and come to stand before the divine throne. Yet, with the single exception of the soul in the Apocalypse of Zephaniah, there is no indication that any of the heroes are actually in danger despite their reaction to their awesome surroundings. After all, these heroes have been taken up to heaven at God's initiative; if God had not considered them worthy, they would not be there. In contrast to the apocalypses, the hekhalot texts provide instructions that at least in theory permit people to undertake ascent at their own initiative, and both *Hekhalot Rabbati* and *Hekhalot Zutarti* consider the problem of what happens when someone who is not truly worthy of standing before the divine throne chooses to undertake the journey.

The two works describe a pair of tests in very similar terms. The first test makes the concern explicit: its goal is described as determining whether the one who descends to the chariot (even *Hekhalot Zutarti* uses this terminology here) is worthy "to see the king in his beauty." The test consists of an invitation to enter the hekhal; neither work specifies which hekhal. If upon receiving the invitation the visionary enters immediately, he has shown himself unworthy and suffers the violent consequences. A worthy visionary waits until asked a second time (*HR* 258; *HZ* 407).

The second test follows immediately on the first in both *Hekhalot Rabbati* and *Hekhalot Zutarti*. It takes place at the gate of the sixth hekhal, and the pairing of the two tests may suggest that the first test too was understood to take place there. The story of R. Nehuniah ben haQanah in *Hekhalot Rabbati* also treats the sixth hekhal as a particularly dangerous spot, as noted above, but there the danger is not for the visionary himself but for scribes stationed by the visionary to record what he reports about his vision. As the visionary arrives at the gate of the sixth hekhal in the second test of *Hekhalot Rabbati* and *Hekhalot Zutarti*, he is overwhelmed by the sight of "hundreds of thousands of myriads of waves of water." But if he asks about the water, he is revealed as unworthy, as a descendant of those who worshiped the Golden Calf, and is attacked with axes of iron. For what he sees is not water but the brilliance of the pure marble of the sixth hekhal (*HR* 259; *HZ* 408–9). At the conclusion of its version of the second test *Hekhalot Zutarti* offers the remarkable suggestion that as long as the visionary manages to restrain himself and keep silent about the waters, he will survive, whether worthy or not. This claim certainly increases the value of the instructions.

The second test's picture of the danger of misperception in the course of ascent recalls the misperceptions of the visionary in the Apocalypse of Zephaniah, particularly his mistaking a sea of fire for a sea of water, which is quite similar to the mistake that can be so dangerous for the visionary in *Hekhalot Rabbati* and *Hekhalot Zutarti*. Yet despite his repeated mistakes the visionary of the Apocalypse of Zephaniah never comes to harm. Of course, unlike the visionaries of *Hekhalot Rabbati* and *Hekhalot Zutarti*, he is a dead soul; thus it was not his own choice to undertake the journey. What is more, despite his failings, in the end he is found to be worthy, his righteous deeds outnumbering his wicked deeds.

Although they come down to us joined together, it seems likely that the two tests originally circulated separately. To begin with, there is no need for two since either one will have the desired effect. Furthermore, the famous passage in the Babylonian Talmud about the four rabbis who entered paradise (*b. Hagigah* 14b), which pre-dates the composition of *Hekhalot Rabbati and Hekhalot Zutarti* by some time, alludes to the water test but does not mention the invitation. Nor is the relationship of the tests to the instructions in *Hekhalot Rabbati* and *Hekhalot Zutarti* clear. Both tests presuppose the picture of the gates of the hekhalot guarded by angelic gatekeepers found in the instructions, but in neither work do the tests appear in the course of the instructions.

Ascent by Song

Descent by means of seals is not the only technique for approaching the divine throne in *Hekhalot Rabbati*. The work begins with another technique implied in R. Ishmael's question, "What are the songs that one who wishes to look upon the sight of the chariot, to descend in peace and to ascend in peace, should recite?" (*HR* 81). The answer to this question is postponed as the text goes on to describe the practical benefits that attach to such a journey (*HR* 81–93). After this description R. Ishmael asks again, "What is the special quality of the songs a man sings to descend to the chariot?" (*HR* 94). This time the response is a hymn or series of hymns in which the trishagion, "Holy, holy, holy, is the Lord of Hosts" (Isa. 6:3), plays a central role as it does in the prayers of the synagogue. At the conclusion of the hymns R. Ishmael says, "All these songs Rabbi Aqiba heard when he descended to the chariot, and he took hold of them and learned them before the throne of glory, (the songs) that his servants were singing before him" (*HR* 106). According to this passage, then, the way to descend to the chariot is to recite the hymns sung by the angels who stand before it. While *Hekhalot Rabbati*'s version of the instructions examined above makes participation in the angelic liturgy the goal of descent, in this passage it is not only the goal but also the means.

The hymnic material of *Hekhalot Rabbati* and the hekhalot texts more generally has a distinctive style that goes far beyond the parallelism that is the defining feature of biblical poetry to a truly virtuosic piling up of synonyms:

> From the praise and song of every day, from the joy and exultation of every time, and from the sound that comes forth from the mouth of the holy ones, from the melody that rushes forth from the mouth of the ministering angels, mountains of fire and hills of flame, piled up and hidden, given forth every day, as it is said, "Holy, holy, holy, is the Lord of Hosts. The whole earth is full of his glory." (*HR* 95)

The hymns and liturgical compositions found among the Dead Sea Scrolls provide some precedent for the style of the hekhalot hymns. There is even some overlap in their vocabularies, probably due to their biblical sources:

> The seat of your honor and the footstools of your glory in the heights where you reside, and the dwelling of your holiness and the chariots of your glory, their cherubim and ophanim and all their councils, foundations of fire and flames of brightness, splendors of beauty ... (4Q286)

Aspects of the hymns of the hekhalot texts also find parallels in the apocalypses. The two apocalypses that provide the most detail about the heavenly liturgy, the Parables of Enoch and the book of Revelation, give the trishagion a central place. The song Abraham recites for protection in the course of his ascent in the Apocalypse of Abraham also shows similarities to the hymns of the hekhalot texts. It shares the hekhalot hymns' love of synonyms, though the vocabulary is significantly different: "Eternal One, Mighty One, Holy One, El god, Monarch, Self-begotten, incorruptible, unsullied, unborn, immaculate, immortal, self-perfect, self-illuminated, Without mother, without father, without birth, the High One, the Fiery One" (Apoc. Abr. 17:7–9). Of course, though the Apocalypse of Abraham was probably written in Hebrew, it reaches us only in a Slavonic translation made from an intermediate Greek translation; thus the hymn surely underwent significant change in the process. The idea of songs serving as protection in the course of ascent appears clearly in a passage in another one of the hekhalot texts, *Ma'aseh Merkavah*, in which R. Nehuniah ben haQanah teaches R. Ishmael five songs to recite to keep himself safe in the course of descent and ascent (*MM* 586–91). These songs combine repetitious but pious praise of God that would be at home in the synagogue with long lists of divine names. Here it appears that the protective power of the songs resides in the power of the names; that is, the songs are a kind of magical spell. Finally, it is worth recalling the striking parallel noted above: both in the Apocalypse of Abraham and the instructions of *Hekhalot Rabbati* the visionary sings the song of the throne.

Instructions and Practice

In contrast to the ascent apocalypses, which narrate the stories of ancient heroes who are taken up to heaven at God's initiative, the hekhalot texts provide instructions that claim to enable their readers to reach the chariot-throne at their own initiative. But there is reason to be cautious about viewing the hekhalot works as reflecting a practice of ascent among Jews in the post-rabbinic era. One striking piece of evidence that undercuts a straightforward reading of the instructions as guidance for those undertaking ascent comes at the end of the instructions in *Hekhalot Zutarti*. After the instructions have deposited the adept in God's lap and provided him with the prayer for binding angels to do his will, they continue: "Repeat this mishnah every day after prayer" (*HZ* 419).

This unexpected conclusion to the instructions suggests that their real purpose is not to enable anyone who wishes to undertake a journey to the divine throne but rather to provide a substitute for the journey, a way of achieving the benefits it confers without actually undertaking it. In a passage that comes shortly after the instruction to repeat the mishnah every day, R. Aqiba reports on a divine voice that promises to redeem the household in which a blessing for those who ascend to the chariot is repeated and decrees forty days of fasting before the recitation, which must be undertaken in a state of sexual purity with the head between the knees (*HZ* 424). Supplementing the recitation with ritual preparation serves to underline its significance and make it a worthy substitute for ascent.

This understanding of the purpose of the instructions does not apply to *Hekhalot Rabbati*, where there is no call to recite the instructions, and, as we have seen, the first set of instructions does provide directions for beginning the process of descent. But *Hekhalot Rabbati* includes one unit in which recitation plays a significant role. The procedure for adjuring the Prince of the Torah, the angel who can make scholars of Torah immune to forgetting, consists of a process of purification, isolation, and fasting for twelve days, together with recitation of the account of the origin of the ritual, which the passage has just provided, and finally standing and calling on various angels twelve times (*HR* 299–300). Thus it is not impossible that the instructions for descent in *Hekhalot Rabbati* should also be understood as intended for recitation rather than performance. In any case, the evidence of *Hekhalot Zutarti* suggests that the gap between the presentation of ascent in the apocalypses on the one hand and the hekhalot texts on the other is smaller than it first appears.

3 Enoch (*Sefer Hekhalot*)

Although 3 Enoch shares some of the central interests of the other hekhalot works, such as the angelic hierarchy and the angelic liturgy, it differs from them in a number of ways. Much of 3 Enoch, for example, refers to the levels of the divine realm not as hekhalot (or palaces) but as heavens. The relatively orderly arrangement and integration of once independent units in 3 Enoch reflects a stronger editorial hand than is evident in the other hekhalot works, and the greater coherence of its content clearly reflects the editors' selectivity. The editors chose to exclude any material that smacks of magic; thus 3 Enoch contains no instructions for adjuring angels, nor does it contain instructions for ascent, though it does offer narrative accounts of ascents. The editors also include a great deal of material known from rabbinic literature, making 3 Enoch the hekhalot work most in tune with classical rabbinic ideas.

The title "3 Enoch" was conferred on the work by modern scholars; the manuscripts refer to the text as *Sefer Hekhalot*, the

Book of Hekhalot. But the modern title is useful in pointing to one of the most striking differences between this work and the other hekhalot texts: the prominent role of a biblical hero. Rabbi Ishmael, well established as a hero of hekhalot literature, serves as the narrator of 3 Enoch, but virtually everything he reports is revealed to him by Metatron, the angel who is God's second in command here and elsewhere in rabbinic literature and the hekhalot texts. Indeed Metatron's status is so exalted that it caused some anxiety, as is evident in a passage in 3 Enoch that is dependent on a famous story in the Babylonian Talmud. This story reports an incident in which a great rabbi ascends to heaven, sees Metatron enthroned, and as a result becomes a heretic, concluding that there are "two powers in heaven"; in response, God punishes Metatron with lashes and takes away his throne, leaving him to stand.

What makes Metatron's status in 3 Enoch's version of his career even more remarkable is that, as he reveals to R. Ishmael, he was not always an angel; rather, he began life as the patriarch Enoch. The apocalypses have given us some preparation for this. As far back as the Book of the Watchers, Enoch proves to be the equal of the angels, while in the Parables of Enoch he is discovered to be the exalted son of man, and in 2 Enoch he is transformed into an angel. But 3 Enoch goes beyond even the Parables and 2 Enoch in its emphasis on how the transformed Enoch outranks the entire angelic hierarchy.

Despite the significant structural similarities, common interests, and occasional similarity of detail, there is nothing in the hekhalot works other than 3 Enoch to suggest textual connection to the ascent apocalypses. There are very significant differences in their concerns, and the similarities appear to reflect a shared interest in the interpretation of particular biblical passages such as Isaiah 6 and Ezekiel 1 and common features of the ancient Jewish worldview. For 3 Enoch, the situation is different. The patriarch Enoch does not play a major role in classical rabbinic literature, and 3 Enoch can hardly be understood without reference to the apocalyptic tradition. How the authors of the Metatron section of 3 Enoch arrived at this knowledge is an open question, though one scholar has recently made a persuasive case that the work reflects knowledge of the story of the descent of the watchers, probably by way of Greek excerpts preserved in the world history of George Syncellos, a ninth-century Byzantine monk.

Syncellos' work, however, cannot account for the exaltation of Enoch in 3 Enoch. Yet while we remain ignorant of the channels by which traditions about the exaltation of Enoch reached 3 Enoch, it is hard to avoid the conclusion that the placement of a transformed human figure as the second highest being in the universe reflects at least to some extent the authors' encounter with Christianity. The transformation of Enoch into Metatron constitutes an embrace of a Christian idea that must have been very attractive, the idea that a human being could become divine, but it substitutes a biblical hero already associated with life in heaven for Jesus of Nazareth.

Chapter 7

Eschatology
in the Byzantine Empire

For 4 Ezra and the book of Revelation at the end of the first century, the Roman empire was the last beast of the book of Daniel. Not much more than two centuries later, the beast had embraced Christianity, and Christians were no longer a persecuted minority sect but adherents of the imperial religion. For Jews, on the other hand, those two centuries were a particularly difficult period. The revolt against Rome that caused the destruction of the Second Temple in 70 CE was followed by a second revolt in 132–5, whose leader, Simeon bar Koziba, called himself "bar Kokhba," "son of a star," a title that appears to reflect a messianic interpretation of a passage in the book of Numbers (Num. 24:17). The coins minted by Bar Kokhba and some comments in rabbinic literature lend support to the view that the revolt had a messianic agenda. The timing of the revolt may have been inspired in part by the passage of almost seventy years since the destruction of the Second Temple; the Second Temple, after all, had been dedicated seventy years after the destruction of the First Temple. Surely the very idea that the Jews could succeed in throwing off the yoke of Rome reflected the expectation of divine intervention on their behalf. The consequences of the Bar Kokhba Revolt were if anything more devastating than those of the first revolt. The Jewish population of Judea was decimated, and Jews were forbidden to live in Jerusalem, which the Romans turned into the pagan city of Aelia Capitolina.

Despite these setbacks, until the beginning of the fourth century Jews were one minority among many in the multi-cultural Roman empire. But in 313, with its public adoption by Constantine, Christianity became the dominant religion of the empire. In the wake of this development Jews found themselves in a new position of vulnerability. Before Constantine, Jews and Christians could argue on equal terms over how to read their shared scriptures or who was the true Israel; indeed, as adherents of a legal religion Jews usually had a certain advantage over Christians in the eyes of the imperial authorities despite the calamities of the two revolts. But with Constantine's embrace of Christianity the rivalry between Jews and Christians was decisively resolved in favor of Christians. Thus it is not surprising that Jews seem to have experienced another burst of eschatological hope during the brief reign of the emperor Julian "the Apostate" (361–3), who, as part of his effort to roll back the Christianization of the empire, authorized the rebuilding of the Temple. But his untimely death in battle against the Persians brought a decisive end to his project, much to the relief of Christians.

The failure of the two revolts left the rabbis, the religious elite of the post-destruction period, cautious about the dangers of intense eschatological expectation, and, unlike many Jews, they appear to have been skeptical about Julian's attempt to rebuild the Temple. But this caution does not mean that they had abandoned the hope of redemption, only that they were suspicious of men who claimed to be its agents, and there is a considerable body of eschatological speculation in rabbinic literature of the first five centuries of the Christian era, though none of it takes the form of an apocalypse.

Sefer Zerubbabel

Jewish eschatological hopes were aroused once again early in the seventh century. In the first decades of the century the wars between Persia and Byzantium threatened the Christian hold on the Holy Land and the holy city. *Sefer Zerubbabel*, the Book of Zerubbabel, perhaps the most influential of the medieval Jewish apocalypses, reflects the eschatological hopes raised by the Persian conquest of Jerusalem in 614. By the beginning of the seventh century Jerusalem had been a Christian city for almost 300 years, and Christians were shocked by its loss to the Persians, which threatened the Christian identity of the city: the Church of the Holy Sepulcher, the most important church in the city, was damaged by fire, and the Persians also removed its most revered relic, the Holy Cross. But the Persian triumph did not last long. In 628 the Byzantine emperor Heraclius defeated the Persians, and in 630 he arranged a dramatic restoration of the Holy Cross to the Church of the Holy Sepulcher. But this reversal too was short-lived. From 638 Jerusalem was ruled neither by Byzantines nor by Persians but by the Muslim invaders, the newest force in the area. *Sefer Zerubbabel*'s eschatological scenario describes the struggle between the kings of Christendom and the kings of Persia, but it is unaware of the Muslims; thus *Sefer Zerubbabel* should be dated sometime before the Muslim conquest.

Sefer Zerubbabel is often referred to as an apocalypse, and the designation is in some ways appropriate: its subject is the coming of the messiah, or rather messiahs, and it takes as its protagonist a figure whose association with the rebuilding of the Second Temple makes him a suitable hero for a work concerned with the manifestation (I choose this term advisedly) of the Third Temple. The choice of a biblical figure is particularly noteworthy in light of the preference of the not much later hekhalot texts for rabbis as heroes. Nonetheless it is unlikely that the author of *Sefer Zerubbabel* was aware of the apocalypse as a genre. Although *Sefer Zerubbabel* clearly made use of Daniel, the author would not have identified it as an apocalypse, for despite the scholarly categorization the term does not appear in Daniel or elsewhere in the Jewish canon, and there is no clear Hebrew equivalent for it. If there is a biblical model for the diverse elements that make up *Sefer Zerubbabel*, it is probably the book of Ezekiel; *Sefer Zerubbabel* is also deeply indebted to other prophetic books, particularly Isaiah and Zechariah.

Sefer Zerubbabel opens with Zerubbabel praying as he broods over the destruction of the Temple. In response to the prayer, God takes Zerubbabel to the city of "Rome," here used for the Byzantine capital, Constantinople. Here Zerubbabel meets a man of humble appearance, wounded and suffering, who, to Zerubbabel's amazement, turns into a handsome young man who is the Davidic messiah, Menahem ben Amiel. While Menahem appears as a name for the messiah in the Babylonian Talmud and elsewhere in rabbinic literature, the patronymic ben Amiel first appears here. An angel identified as both Michael and Metatron, each a name for the leading angel in the angelic hierarchy, arrives to reveal to Zerubbabel some of the events of the last days. Hephzibah, the mother of the Davidic messiah, will kill the evil kings of Yemen and Antioch with the help of a wondrous staff that God had originally given to Adam. After five years she will be joined by Nehemiah ben Hushiel, the messiah descended from Joseph; this name does not appear before *Sefer Zerubbabel*. Nehemiah will gather the people of Israel together. Then Shiroi, king of Persia, will attack, and Hephzibah will slay him as well.

Next Zerubbabel learns about Rome's part in the eschatological drama. The angel takes Zerubbabel to a "house of disgrace and merrymaking," apparently a church, where he shows him a beautiful stone statue of a virgin who becomes pregnant by Satan and gives birth to Armilos, the eschatological opponent of the Jews. Only after Armilos has slain Nehemiah will the Davidic messiah arrive on the scene, accompanied by Elijah the prophet. The two of them will bring Nehemiah back to life, and together with them Hephzibah and Nehemiah will bring salvation to the Jews as the dead are resurrected. The Davidic messiah will kill Armilos, and finally God himself will descend to fight the eschatological enemies, Gog and Magog and the forces of Armilos. Then an enormous temple made in heaven will descend to earth. The work concludes with a different account of the eschatological wars, which also culminates in the death of Armilos at the hands of the Davidic messiah and includes a description of Armilos that belongs to a genre of descriptions of the Antichrist found in both Jewish and Christian texts.

While this summary gives a good idea of the content of *Sefer Zerubbabel*, it suggests a more coherent narrative than the book actually provides. Its author was as much an editor and a compiler as an author. Like the hekhalot texts, *Sefer Zerubbabel* is composed of a number of separable and loosely integrated units, of which some clearly had an independent existence. But unlike the hekhalot texts, *Sefer Zerubbabel* is primarily a narrative, making the loose integration of the various units more jarring. Thus, for example, the messiah descended from David makes his appearance twice, first in the course of an eschatological timetable, and then again at the end of the timetable, where he arrives together with Elijah and the messiah descended from Joseph. It is equally anticlimactic when, after the culmination of the eschatological scenario including God's appearance and the descent of the Third Temple, the text provides an alternate version of the eschatological wars.

Yet despite the loosely integrated sources, the major concerns of *Sefer Zerubbabel* emerge clearly. It is the first apocalyptic work with historical interests considered here to have been written in the shadow of a Christian empire, and it offers a remarkable indication of the fascination certain aspects of Christianity held for at least some Jews. For example, it is at once attracted and repelled by the figure of the Virgin Mary. The feeling of repulsion is evident in the role of the stone statue of a virgin as an important member of the forces of evil, the sexual partner of Satan and the mother of the Jewish version of the Antichrist. But *Sefer Zerubbabel* cannot deny that the statue is very beautiful. Indeed, the attraction exercised by the Virgin Mary is so strong that *Sefer Zerubbabel* provides a mother for the Davidic messiah and gives her a central role.

The role Hephzibah plays in *Sefer Zerubbabel* is rather surprising. Although she is identified as the mother of the Davidic messiah, she is never shown in a maternal role, nor does she intercede with God on behalf of the Jewish people as the Virgin was understood to intercede on behalf of Christians. Rather, Hephzibah is a warrior who appears with the messiah son of Joseph at her side. But even this most unmotherly role reflects the function of the Virgin Mary in contemporary Byzantium, where, from the late sixth to early eighth century, images of the Virgin were taken into battle to ensure victory, or painted on the walls of the city for protection. Thus, while the figure of Hephzibah subverts some central aspects of the character of the Virgin Mary as the Christian neighbors of the author of the *Sefer Zerubbabel* understood her, even the subversion is indebted to contemporary Christian ideas and imagery.

Sefer Zerubbabel marks both the beginning and the end of Hephzibah's career. Though many Jewish apocalyptic works written after the rise of the Islam are deeply indebted to *Sefer Zerubbabel*, finding a place for Nehemiah ben Hushiel, Armilos, and even the stone statue in their eschatological scenarios, they ignore Hephzibah. This omission may reflect an understanding of the figure of the mother of the messiah as a defining difference between Judaism and Christianity: she belongs to Christians, not Jews. But it is also possible that for Jews writing under Muslim rule the Virgin Mary no longer provoked such an intense reaction. Thus they retain the stone statue, which mocks Christian beliefs, but leave out the figure of Hephzibah, which provides a Jewish equivalent for the mother of the messiah.

Another feature of Christianity that seems to have captured the imagination of the author of *Sefer Zerubbabel* is the idea of a suffering messiah. This idea is certainly not unprecedented in Jewish sources; indeed, the suffering servant poems that appear in a portion of the book of Isaiah written in the sixth century BCE are a crucial source for shaping the earliest perceptions of the suffering of Jesus. The suffering servant also shapes the depiction of the suffering Davidic messiah in a famous passage from the Babylonian Talmud (*b. Sanhedrin* 98a) and in *Sefer Zerubbabel* itself, as is clear not only from the imagery but from specific vocabulary. In addition, both the Talmud and *Sefer Zerubbabel* describe the messiah living incognito at the gates of Rome, that is, Constantinople. This shared feature certainly does not derive from the book of Isaiah, which did not know of Rome. But *Sefer Zerubbabel*'s picture does not include the most striking detail found in the Talmud, the messiah's unbinding his wounds and binding them again one by one so as always to be in readiness for his mission, suggesting that its picture does not derive from the Talmud's but from a tradition on which the Talmud also drew.

Even if the Babylonian Talmud and *Sefer Zerubbabel* drew on biblical sources for their picture of the suffering messiah, the centrality of suffering for the Christian understanding of the messiah surely encouraged their development of such a picture. The impact of Christianity is even clearer in *Sefer Zerubbabel*'s adaptation of the death and resurrection of the messiah. But it is not the Davidic messiah, the dominant figure in the eschatological scenario, who dies and comes back to life in *Sefer Zerubbabel*. Rather, it is the other messiah, the messiah descended from Joseph, whose death is also mentioned, though very briefly, in the Babylonian Talmud.

The idea of two messiahs is not an innovation of the rabbinic era. As we have seen, the pairing of a royal messiah with a priestly messiah goes back as far as the early Second Temple period and the prophet Zechariah, and it is the dominant messianic picture of the Dead Sea Scrolls. This pairing, however, has a different significance from the pairing of messiahs descended from David and Joseph. King David came from the tribe of Judah, and his descendants ruled over the southern Israelite kingdom, also known as Judah, from the tenth century BCE to the Babylonian conquest in the early sixth century BCE. The larger and more prosperous Israelite kingdom, known as Israel, was shorter-lived; it was conquered by the Assyrians in 722 BCE. Unlike the southern kingdom, the northern kingdom was ruled by many different dynasties, but the dominant tribe among the ten that made up the kingdom was the tribe of Ephraim. Ephraim and his brother Manasseh were Joseph's sons, adopted by the patriarch Jacob, their grandfather, on his death-bed in order to give Joseph, his favorite son, a double portion among his brothers. Thus the presence in Jewish eschatology of a messiah descended from Joseph alongside the Davidic messiah reflects the desire for the restoration of the people of Israel to its original composition, with the long-lost ten tribes rejoining the descendants of the inhabitants of the kingdom of Judah.

Sefer Zerubbabel's division of aspects of the career of the Christian messiah between the Davidic messiah and the messiah descended from Joseph recalls its division of aspects of the character and function of the Virgin Mary between two figures, the beautiful statue and the warrior Hephzibah. Of course, both of the messiahs are positive figures while the statue is certainly not. *Sefer Zerubbabel* may have inherited the association of suffering with the Davidic messiah, thus predetermining which messiah would be associated with suffering. In any case, the decision to attribute death and resurrection to the secondary messiah rather than the primary one might have helped to defuse any anxiety that the death and resurrection to a Jewish messiah caused *Sefer Zerubbabel*'s audience. Whatever the author's intention, his innovation was received with enthusiasm, for, as already noted, unlike Hephzibah, Nehemiah becomes a common figure in later eschatological scenarios.

Sefer Eliyyahu

I have already noted that *Sefer Zerubbabel* differs from the roughly contemporary hekhalot literature in taking as its hero not a great rabbi but, in the style of Second Temple-era apocalypses, a biblical figure. Nor does its style owe much to rabbinic practice. The absence of rabbinic influence can be seen clearly when *Sefer Zerubbabel* is compared to *Sefer Eliyyahu*, the Book of Elijah, the other Jewish work with apocalyptic interests written in response to the events of the early seventh century.

Sefer Eliyyahu is a brief work, perhaps three pages in Hebrew, but despite its brevity it consists of several separate units that are at best loosely connected in their present context. It opens with the passage from 1 Kings 19 that describes Elijah's flight to Mount Horeb after his defeat of the priests of Ba'al on Mount Carmel, yet it goes on to attribute the contents of the work to a revelation by the archangel Michael to Elijah on Mount Carmel. There follows a very brief account of the spirit of the Lord carrying Elijah to three of the four corners of the earth, where he sees sights reminiscent of those in Enoch's tour to the ends of the earth in the Book of the Watchers; the similarities are difficult to account for since there is no reason to believe that the Book of the Watchers was available in Aramaic or even in Greek in seventh-century Palestine or Asia Minor. After the tour Michael reveals the name of the last king, a name that marks him as a Roman. But the work goes on to cite the opinions of several rabbis, each of whom gives a different name for the king. The name finally declared to be correct is Persian. Next comes a brief report on the war between Rome and Persia, followed by a description of the terrible appearance of the last king of Rome.

There follows a considerably longer unit, a timetable of ten eschatological events, all placed on the twentieth or the twenty-fifth of various months and described in passages of unequal length; it is worth noting that a section of *Sefer Zerubbabel* also relates the events of the eschaton to days of the month. In the course of the timetable the messiah makes his appearance. The events of the timetable are only loosely connected to preceding units of *Sefer Eliyyahu*; for example, Persia and its wars against Rome play no part at all in them.

The concluding section of *Sefer Eliyyahu*, also of some length, at least relatively speaking, consists of five visions, each introduced by the words, "Elijah said, 'I see ....'" The visions describe the last phases of the eschatological drama, but the messiah is strikingly absent. Instead the visions culminate in the descent of the heavenly Jerusalem. The similarities to the book of Revelation, which also concludes with the descent of the heavenly Jerusalem in the course of a series of visions that begin, "I saw," are unlikely to be accidental. Rather, the heavenly Jerusalem of *Sefer Eliyyahu* seems to be a response to that of Revelation. Like the earthly Jerusalem of the seventh century, Revelation's New Jerusalem lacks both temple and Jews. The visions of *Sefer Eliyyahu* insist on the presence of both.

Like *Sefer Zerubbabel*, *Sefer Eliyyahu* takes a biblical figure rather than a rabbi as its hero, yet the influence of rabbinic culture on *Sefer Eliyyahu* is evident in many ways. Thus, as already noted, *Sefer Eliyyau* provides multiple possibilities for the name of the last king, each attributed to a different rabbi. Such presentation of multiple possibilities is standard in rabbinic legal and exegetical discussion, although it is certainly a bit disconcerting in the context of an eschatological scenario. *Sefer Eliyyahu* goes on to resolve the question in typical rabbinic style by decreeing that the "halakhah" or law is in accordance with the words of Rabbi Simeon.

Sefer Eliyyahu is also replete with prooftexts, quotations of biblical verses that rabbinic texts use to support claims of any kind. The verses are introduced with standard rabbinic formulae, usually, "as it is said." Like apocalypses of the Second Temple period, *Sefer Zerubbabel* is deeply informed by passages from the prophetic books of the Bible, but it contains only four actual quotations of biblical verses, of which only two are introduced by a citation formula known from rabbinic literature.

Finally, it is worth noting one more difference between the two apocalypses in their attitude toward rabbinic culture. When the final vision of *Sefer Eliyyahu* describes the dwelling places of the righteous in the New Jerusalem, it also notes the contents of the treasuries of the new temple: Torah and peace. *Sefer Zerubbabel's* eschatological scenario also includes the descent to earth of a heavenly temple, but there is no mention of Torah in its treasuries. The account of the Davidic messiah's encounter with the "elders and sages" is also suggestive; it should be noted that "sages" is a rabbinic self-designation. The elders and sages fail to recognize the messiah because of his humble appearance, and they despise him just as Zerubbabel did on first seeing him. The explicit comparison of the failure of the elders and sages to that of Zerubbabel tempers the criticism somewhat, but if *Sefer Zerubbabel* is not anti-rabbinic, it clearly does not identify the rabbis of the past or the present as the most significant leaders of the Jewish people. In the end, however, *Sefer Zerubbabel's* compelling narrative and attractive heroes were more important than its distance from rabbinic culture. It had a major impact on later apocalyptic works, which are much more rabbinic in style and content, and on liturgical poetry, while *Sefer Eliyyahu*, despite its more rabbinic style, left few traces in later literature.

Eschatology in a Christian Empire

At the beginning of the fourth century Christians were still liable to persecution under Roman law. But while the rapid and dramatic change of status brought about by Constantine's embrace of Christianity made eschatological hopes less urgent, it by no means brought an end to them. After all, the expectation of Christ's return and the new age it will bring is central to Christian teaching. I focus here on Christians in the Byzantine empire, where the Jewish works just discussed were likely written, but Christian eschatological expectations were equally lively in the Latin West.

Eschatological expectations became particularly intense, as might be expected, at moments of crisis caused by natural disaster or war, but also at the approach of years imbued with chronological significance. For example, the approach of the year 500 since the incarnation, which was understood by many as the year 6000 from the creation of the world as well and so the transition from the first six thousand-year "days" to the thousand-year Sabbath, heightened eschatological expectation among Christians. Later the approach of the year 880 had a similar effect. As for natural disaster, the contemporary historian Agathias describes the widespread fear and sense of eschatological doom in response to the earthquakes that shook Constantinople in 557 and 558, causing the collapse of the main dome of the great church of Hagia Sophia. But the event that seems to have done the most to inspire Byzantine Christians to write apocalypses was the Muslim invasion and its aftermath, which saw the first sustained loss of territory and power by the eastern Roman empire since it had become Christian.

The first half of the seventh century was a time of great turmoil in the Byzantine empire. As we have already seen, Jerusalem was in Persian hands between 614 and 628. The Christian reconquest lasted until 638, when Jerusalem fell to the Arabs. From the middle of the fourth decade of the seventh century to the middle of the fifth, the Arabs also succeeded in conquering the Persian empire and the Byzantine provinces of Syria and Egypt. By the end of the seventh century the Dome of the Rock stood on the Temple Mount, a physical expression of Muslim rule in the holy city.

The decades after the Muslim conquest saw the composition of a significant body of Christian apocalypses. One recurring theme of these works is the four-kingdom schema of the book of Daniel and the place of their empire in it; several of the works are attributed to Daniel. According to Daniel 2 and 7, the four kingdoms that were to rule the world before the eschatological kingdom of the holy ones of the Most High were Babylonia, Medea, Persia, and Greece, or rather the empire founded by Alexander. But the author of 4 Ezra, writing only two and a half centuries after the author of Daniel, knew very well that the fourth and last world empire was not Alexander's since that empire had long since been replaced by that of the Romans. Thus he provides Ezra with his own vision of the four kingdoms in which the final kingdom is represented as an eagle, the symbol of Rome, and God himself revises Daniel's vision: "The eagle which you saw coming up from the sea is the fourth kingdom which appeared in a vision to your brother Daniel. But it was not explained to him as I now explain or have explained it to you" (4 Ezra 12:11–12). At the end of the seventh century the Armenian historian Sebeos offers a new interpretation of Daniel 7: the fourth beast represents the kingdom of Ishmael.

But even before the coming of the Arabs Daniel's vision posed a problem for Christian interpreters. Could the fourth beast of Daniel's vision, the most vicious of the four evil empires, really symbolize Rome now that it had become Christian? One line of thought saw the Roman empire as beyond the scope of Daniel's prophecy, which was fulfilled, like all prophecy, by the time of Christ. Other interpreters solved the problem by ignoring the negative depiction of the world empires and concentrating on the positive implications of the fourth position: Roman rule would come to an end not with the triumph of another human empire but with the coming of the divine kingdom.

The Apocalypse of Pseudo-Methodius

The problem of the four kingdoms plays a prominent role in the Apocalypse of Pseudo-Methodius, the most influential Christian apocalypse of the Byzantine era, written sometime during the last two decades of the seventh century. As the name by which it is known to scholars indicates, the apocalypse was attributed not to Daniel or another biblical hero but to Methodius, a learned bishop of Olympus, active at the end of the third and beginning of the fourth century and reputed to have died as a martyr. The work places the revelation to Methodius on the mountain of Singara, territory that had been under Persian rule before the Arab conquest. Since Singara is not otherwise associated with Methodius, it may have been the place where the work was composed. The original language of Pseudo-Methodius was Syriac, but it was soon translated into both Greek and Latin.

Methodius was not the only Church Father to be put to pseude-pigraphic use for apocalyptic purposes. An apocalyptic sermon, probably from the end of the sixth or beginning of the seventh century, preserved in Latin but perhaps originally composed in Syriac, is attributed to the great fourth-century Syrian Father Ephrem, while a later work that includes extracts from Pseudo-Methodius is attributed to John Chrysostom, active in the late fourth and early fifth centuries. The attribution of these works to Church Fathers is comparable to the attribution of contemporary Jewish works such as the hekhalot texts and the apocalyptic works to be discussed below to rabbis of the period of the Mishnah. From the vantage point of the seventh century, Church Fathers and rabbis bore the prestige and authority of antiquity just as biblical heroes did, but they had the added attraction of seeming closer to the authors' own concerns and experiences.

Pseudo-Methodius begins with a selective account of the history of the world from Adam and Eve to Alexander the Great, which serves as the platform for a "prophecy" of the Muslim conquest. Despite the importance of the Bible for Pseudo-Methodius, it shows little interest in the heroes of the Old Testament. Rather, the ancient hero who receives the most attention is Alexander the Great. Pseudo-Methodius credits him with the imprisonment of the hordes of Gog and Magog in the far north, where they will remain until the eschaton. But more important than this exploit is his role as founder of the last world kingdom of Daniel and also as prototype of the final Christian king.

Yet from the point of view of his role as founder, Alexander's mother is even more important than he. The mother's name according to Pseudo-Methodius is Kushet, and she is the daugh-ter of the king of Ethiopia (*Kush* in Hebrew and Syriac). After the death of the childless Alexander, Kushet, presumably a widow, returns to her father's home, where she is courted by Byzas, the eponymous founder of the city of Byzantium, described by Pseudo-Methodius as king of the Greeks. Kushet marries Byzas, and their daughter Byzantia becomes the wife of Romulus, the king of the Romans. Although Pseudo-Methodius draws exten-sively on other Syriac works such as the *Cave of Treasures* and a Syriac version of the Alexander Legend, Kushet is clearly its own invention; no such tradition about the mother of Alexander appears in earlier works. She creates the genealogical connections that allow Pseudo-Methodius to claim that Ethiopia, Macedonia, Greece, and Rome are really one kingdom. Thus the book of Daniel's identification of the fourth kingdom as the Hellenistic empire founded by Alexander does not require updating, since both the Roman empire and the "kingdom of the Greeks," which for Pseudo-Methodius means the Byzantine empire, should be understood as the continuation of Alexander's empire. The Byzantine empire is thus destined to be the last world empire before the end of history.

Furthermore, Kushet's Ethiopian ancestry permits Pseudo-Methodius to read Psalm 68:31 (in the Hebrew Bible 68:32), as describing the role of the Byzantine emperor in the eschatological drama. The verse in question, "Let Ethiopia hasten to stretch out her hands to God," is part of a description of the gifts kings will bring to the Temple in Jerusalem after God's ultimate triumph. The Syriac translation of the verse, however, can be read to say, "Ethiopia will hand over dominion to God."

Pseudo-Methodius criticizes those who believe that the verse in question refers to Ethiopia itself rather than to the "kingdom of Greece." It goes on to work out the implications of the verse in light of 1 Corinthians 15:24, "Then comes the end, when he delivers the kingdom to God the Father after destroying every rule and every authority and power." While it is clear from the context that the antecedent of "he" is Christ, Pseudo-Methodius' paraphrase of the verse has the *son* hand over the *kingdom of the Christians* to God the Father. The paraphrase thus implies that the verse refers not to Christ but to the king of the Christians, the Byzantine emperor. In other words, Pseudo-Methodius takes 1 Corinthians 15:24 to offer the same message as Psalm 68:31: the Byzantine empire will endure until the very end; once it has vanquished all its enemies, its ruler will hand over dominion to God. These enemies include the sons of Ishmael, whose defeat is described in detail later in the work.

Pseudo-Methodius's reading of Daniel is clearly intended to encourage Christians as they confront the successes of their new antagonists, the Arabs. The Muslim invaders do not constitute a new world empire, Pseudo-Methodius insists; they will trouble the Romans for ten weeks of years in the last millennium, but they will eventually be defeated. Furthermore, the sons of Ishmael have been able to triumph over the Christians only because of the sexual sins of the Christians, among which Pseudo-Methodius emphasizes prostitution and homosexuality, both male and female, including even transvestite homosexual prostitution.

The rule of the Muslims, according to this *ex eventu* – after the fact – prophecy, will be oppressive indeed. The new ruler will be a tyrant who enslaves both men and beasts and extracts the poll tax from orphans, widows, and holy men. The allusion to the poll tax may reflect changes in policy toward the end of the seventh century that at once increased the tax on non-Muslims and exempted converts to Islam from the tax; these changes would help to explain Pseudo-Methodius' evident anxiety about the attraction of conversion to Islam.

The new ruler's followers too are described as evil and rapacious: they will take no pity on the poor and will not do justice to the oppressed, but will plunder and afflict the conquered, dash infants to pieces, and kill priests, taking their vestments for their own use. So dire will conditions become under Muslim rule that many Christians will abandon the church of their own accord, without the threat of force, and go over to the Muslims. The destitution of the Christians will cause their oppressors to exclaim, "The Christians have no redeemer!" But this taunt will rouse the king of Greece to action. He will suddenly rise up, defeat the Muslims, and punish the apostates.

With the whole world at peace, the next stage of the eschatological drama will unfold. The gates of the north will open, and the people of Gog and Magog will come forth to wreak havoc on the earth until God sends an angel to destroy them. Now the final evil will be unleashed: the son of perdition will appear in the Holy Land. At last the moment has arrived for the fulfillment of the prophecy of Psalm 68:31. The king of the Greeks will go up to Golgotha, where the cross on which Christ was crucified will again stand, and place his crown atop the cross. This procedure is apparently modeled on a scene from the Syriac *Romance of Julian the Apostate*, in which Jovian is acclaimed emperor by the troops on Julian's death. Jovian insists that they publicly renounce paganism and embrace Christianity. The troops agree, and Jovian takes the cross the army has used as a standard and places the crown on top of it. Jovian offers a prayer, and the crown miraculously descends from the cross on to Jovian's head. In Pseudo-Methodius, once the last king has placed his crown on the cross, he will reach out his hands to heaven to return dominion to God and the cross will ascend to heaven. Then the king will give up his soul to God and the Antichrist will establish himself in Jerusalem, claiming to be God. Finally Christ will return, consigning the Antichrist to hell and admitting the righteous to the kingdom of heaven.

Pseudo-Methodius' message about the Muslim conquest is clear. Christians should take comfort: the end of Muslim power was near, and the Byzantine empire would live on until the very last days. To be sure, it must have been difficult to look forward to the coming of the Antichrist with much enthusiasm, but the evils of the last days were a necessary prelude to the coming of Christ, and for the pious Christians a happy ending was assured. Thus, despite the temptation posed by the possibility of joining the conquerors, there were not only spiritual but practical benefits to remaining loyal to the church.

The central role of the cross in the eschatological drama of Pseudo-Methodius is particularly significant because at the time Pseudo-Methodius was written Jerusalem was no longer in Christian hands. Indeed it is possible that the construction of the Dome of the Rock at the end of the seventh century was one of the events that motivated the author to write his apocalypse. The emphasis on the presence of the cross would thus constitute a response to efforts to remake Jerusalem as a Muslim holy city.

Scholars have struggled to explain the prominence of Ethiopia in Pseudo-Methodius' eschatological schema. Some have suggested that the author felt a particular kinship for Ethiopia because Ethiopians and most Syriac-speaking Christians of the Byzantine empire held a Monophysite Christology, the belief that Christ had only a single, divine nature, even after the condemnation of this position by the Council of Chalcedon in 451. But, as we have seen, there is some reason to believe that Pseudo-Methodius was written in formerly Persian territory, where only a minority of the Christians though they spoke Syriac were Monophysites. On the other hand, Singara itself, where the work may have been written, seems to have been a center of Monophysitism. This complicated situation has led to the suggestion that though the author was not himself a Monophysite, he gave Ethiopia a central role in his work as a way to appeal to Monophysites. But it is important to note that, despite the importance of Ethiopia, Pseudo-Methodius has nothing to say about Christology, Monophysite or otherwise. In the dire circumstances of the Muslim conquest, disagreements about Christology might not have seemed very important, and the role of Ethiopia in Pseudo-Methodius may have nothing to do with Monophysitism. Pseudo-Methodius's insistence that the two Christian kingdoms of Ethiopia and Greece are really one may simply reflect a desire for Christian unity, bringing together the much-diminished Byzantine empire with the only independent Christian kingdom of any size that existed alongside it.

The Impact of Pseudo-Methodius and Jewish Apocalyptic Responses to the Muslim Conquest

The message of Pseudo-Methodius must have been compelling, for it was soon translated into Greek and Latin, and the figure of the last Christian emperor continued to play a significant role in apocalyptic thought in western Europe well into the Middle Ages. But perhaps the best indication of how widely known the figure became is his appearance in the seventh sign in the Signs of Rabbi Simeon bar Yohai, one of several medieval Hebrew lists of ten signs of the coming of the end. Simeon bar Yohai lived in the second century of this era; the Signs is difficult to date, but it clearly postdates the Muslim conquest. It survives in a single manuscript from the Cairo Genizah.

Pseudo-Methodius's account of the last Christian emperor's return of the crown required some revision to make it suitable for a Jewish eschatological scenario. Thus the Signs has the last emperor place the crown not on the cross but on the foundation stone of the Temple, a legendary stone that plays a significant role in rabbinic law and lore. Also, while Pseudo-Methodius's king turns over the crown in silence, the king of the Signs offers an apology for his ancestors' behavior that no Christian would have written: "Master of the Universe, I have now returned to you what my fathers took." The Signs' adaptation of the scene is a striking indication of the ongoing impact on Jews of Christian culture in general and Christian eschatological thought in particular.

The passage from the Signs demonstrates Jewish interest in a scene from a Christian apocalypse written in response to the Muslim conquest. A more direct Jewish response to the conquest can be found in another work attributed to the same rabbinic hero, the Secrets of Rabbi Simeon bar Yohai. The Secrets begins with the angel Metatron revealing the interpretation of several biblical passages that indicate that God intends the Muslim conquest to liberate Jews from the yoke of Christendom. This positive evaluation of the conquest appears to come from the middle of the seventh century, shortly after the event, when Muslim rule could still be seen as a mere prelude to the dawning of the messianic era. The Secrets goes on to prophesy a series of kings, recognizable despite the veiled terms of the description as Muslim rulers to the middle of the eighth century, presumably the date of the final form of the work. Their rule will be followed by a brief period of Christian domination, and then the messianic age will dawn. The eschatological scenario is indebted to *Sefer Zerubbabel* for a number of elements, including the figure of Armilos and an Ephraimite messiah. A century after the Muslim conquest, this portion of the Secrets views Muslim rule much less enthusiastically. While it calls the second Muslim king a friend of Israel, it describes the kings who follow in neutral or negative terms.

At the end of the eleventh century someone composed another work attributed to Rabbi Simeon, the Prayer of Rabbi Simeon bar Yohai. The Prayer adapts portions of the Secrets and combines them with traditions from rabbinic literature and details of *Sefer Zerubbabel* beyond those that appear in the Secrets. The Prayer retains the Secrets' positive evaluation of the second king and continues to treat Christendom as the final enemy, but Muslims are no longer seen as liberators of Israel, and most of the Muslim kings are depicted as harsh rulers. The change in attitude can be seen clearly in the contrast between the rather positive mention of Mohammed in the early portion of the Secrets as a prophet set over the descendants of Ishmael by God and the Prayer's reference to him as a crazy man possessed by a spirit.

Many centuries separate the book of Daniel and the Prayer of Rabbi Simeon, yet readings of contemporary events that detect signs of the imminence of the messianic age continued to find a receptive audience among Jews and Christians well into the Middle Ages. In the final chapter we shall see that the expectations inspired by apocalyptic writings played a significant role in the modern period as well, up to our own time.

Chapter 8

Apocalyptic Movements
in the Modern Era

In late winter and early spring 1993 Americans watched in horrified fascination as the FBI laid siege to a compound occupied by a tiny apocalyptic movement and its messiah in full view of television cameras. The confrontation with a hundred or so Branch Davidians living in a compound they called Mount Carmel outside Waco, Texas, began on February 28, 1993, with a failed raid in response to reports of a cache of firearms. The siege ended in a terrible fire on April 19. Only nine of the Branch Davidians inside the compound survived; seventy-four, including their messiah, David Koresh, died, some from the effects of the fire itself, others, like Koresh, from gunshot wounds that were either self-inflicted or inflicted by members of the group on each other.

The Branch Davidians offer a striking indication of the continued vitality of the ideas discussed in the previous chapters. In some ways, their movement was thoroughly modern. Their heyday preceded the development of the internet, but they made ample use of one of the characteristic media of communication of the late twentieth century, the videocassette. On the other hand, their message was deeply informed by ideas familiar from ancient texts, and interpretation of the two apocalypses in the Christian canon, the books of Daniel and Revelation, played a central role in the movement. In this final chapter I attempt to place the Branch Davidians in a larger context.

By the last centuries of the first millennium the apocalyptic genre was in decline, although the canonical apocalypses remained extremely influential and other apocalyptic works continued to be read and copied. Christians in western Europe reworked the tour of hell from the Apocalypse of Paul late into the Middle Ages, and they also produced new visions of hell, although these were usually attributed to more recent figures rather than the great heroes of the biblical past. Among Jews, the hekhalot texts continued to be copied even as new forms of Jewish mysticism developed. Indeed, there was no lack of visionary activity in the second millennium. But visionaries such as the German abbess Hildegard of Bingen (1098–1179), the English hermit Richard Rolle (first half of the fourteenth century), and Ignatius of Loyola (1491–1556), the founder of the Jesuit order, now spoke in their own names rather than in the name of an ancient hero, and although their visions sometimes conveyed the kind of information found in apocalypses, the conventions of the apocalyptic genre had no impact on the reporting of the visions.

Even during the period when apocalypses flourished, Jews and Christians had used a variety of other genres to express their eschatological expectations or to describe their picture of the heavens. Thus, for example, commentaries, particularly on the book of Revelation but on other biblical works as well, played a central role in the apocalyptic thought of Latin Christians from late antiquity on. In the second millennium, topics central to the ancient apocalypses frequently appeared in sermons, histories, poems, and other genres. The works of Joachim of Fiore (1135–1202), one of the most influential eschatological thinkers of the Middle Ages, are a good example. Against the standard Christian view that history was divided into two stages, before and after Christ, Joachim claimed three stages corresponding to the triune godhead. The third period, already under way in Joachim's lifetime, was the period of the Spirit; in this Sabbath of love and freedom humanity would come to know God more directly than ever before. Joachim even reported having received two revelations, one about the book of Revelation. Yet he presented his innovative theory in treatises involving complex biblical exegesis with a special interest in correlations between the Old Testament and the New.

Apocalyptic Movements

But even as the apocalypse as a literary genre fell into disuse, the ancient apocalypses and their images and ideas maintained their hold on the imagination of Christians. (The role of the ancient apocalypses in Jewish apocalypticism in medieval and modern times is more limited, as we shall see below.) While the apocalypses themselves encourage readers to wait for God or his divine agents to bring an end to history, from antiquity on, many people have not been so patient. The Essenes and the followers of Jesus waited for God's intervention, but Josephus, as we have seen, describes prophets and would-be kings who led large crowds against the Romans with predictably disastrous results (see chapter 4 above). Such movements continued to appear during late antiquity and the early Middle Ages, although often they have left only faint traces in the historical record. They seem to have become more common with the beginning of the second Christian millennium.

Such movements were by no means confined to Jews and Christians. Medieval China, for example, was the scene of a number of movements that drew on Buddhist teachings about Maitreya, the future Buddha who will arrive at the nadir of human history when the teachings of the first Buddha have been forgotten, and inaugurate a new era. Shi'ite Muslims await the return of the twelfth imam, who disappeared in the ninth century, and some scholars have suggested that the behavior of some members of the government in Iran today is aimed at speeding his return. Muhammad Ahmad (1844–85), the religious leader who briefly liberated Sudan from the Egyptians and the British, claimed to be the Mahdi, the divinely guided restorer of the faith according to Sunni Muslims.

In western Europe, during the period of the Crusades, from the end of the eleventh through the thirteenth centuries, many poor people joined the aristocratic warriors who went east to liberate the Holy Land. The result was the pillaging of wealthy towns by these poor hangers-on and the murder of Jews across Europe. But, as Norman Cohn has shown in his classic work, *The Pursuit of the Millennium: Revolutionary Millenarians and Mystical Anarchists of the Middle Ages* (1957), the experience of the Crusades gave the poor a new self-understanding in which they rather than nobles or clerics were God's chosen, an understanding reflected in legends about the crusading "Tafurs" and their king.

During the same period small armies of the poor in various places in Europe attempted to bring about the arrival of the new age. Sometimes their leaders succeeded in attracting a following that went beyond the poor. Some leaders laid claim to the role of the last emperor described in the Apocalypse of Pseudo-Methodius and the works dependent on it that circulated widely in the West. So too popular kings came to be seen as playing that role. The deaths of these kings before they had succeeded in inaugurating the eschaton led to further developments of the legend. One king who inspired great hopes in his subjects was the Holy Roman Emperor Frederick II. When Frederick died in 1250, ten years before the beginning of the eschaton as prophesied by some contemporary sources, some of those who had placed their hopes in him refused to believe that he had actually died, claiming instead that he was concealed in the midst of Mount Etna and would return to reveal himself at the appropriate time.

The dawn of modernity did nothing to bring an end to movements hoping to inaugurate the new era. Indeed, there appears to have been an upsurge in such movements in early modern Europe. As Cohn notes, the Reformation and the spread of literacy may actually have promoted them by validating the individual's own reading of the Bible even as the authority of the church was undermined. The Anabaptists, for example, were more radical critics of the church than Luther himself. They aimed to live by the New Testament and to recreate the communal ethic of the earliest Christian communities. Usually they lived peacefully with their neighbors, but sometimes their ideals led them to attempt to establish the New Jerusalem on earth in anticipation of the coming end. One particularly striking example of Anabaptist apocalypticism was their take-over of Münster, a German town of some size, in 1534–5. The attempt ended in dictatorship and terror under Jan Bockelson, also known as John of Leyden, a failed tailor who became king of the New Jerusalem and announced himself as the messiah. Though Anabaptists admired the church's community of goods, Bockelson lived in extravagant pomp, and he demanded that his subjects, who had advocated a particularly strict sexual morality, practice polygamy. Neighboring rulers were predictably distressed by what they saw in Münster, and when they succeeded in taking the town they killed most of the inhabitants.

The Fifth Monarchists

The middle of the seventeenth century was also a period of heightened eschatological expectations. On the continent, some Protestants understood the success of the century-long struggle of the largely Calvinist northern provinces of the Netherlands to liberate themselves from their Catholic Spanish overlords, ratified in the Peace of Westphalia in 1648, in eschatological terms. So too in England, the turbulent years of civil war in the 1640s were accompanied by an upsurge in eschatological excitement among members of the dissenting churches and even among adherents of the Church of England. With the failure of the millennium to materialize even after the execution of Charles I in 1649, the eschatological excitement began to subside. A few people, however, remained convinced that the end was near even after the Rump Parliament and then Oliver Cromwell proved unwilling to make the radical changes necessary to inaugurate the new era. These people came to be known as Fifth Monarchists after Daniel 7's prophecy of the kingdom of the holy ones of the Most High – "saints" of the Most High in the King James Version – that is to follow on the four evil kingdoms. To the Fifth Monarchists, who came from churches in which membership was presumed to mean salvation and whose members thus referred to themselves as saints, it was clear that Daniel's prophecy was about them.

The outlook of the Fifth Monarchists was deeply informed by the Bible and particularly the books of Daniel and Revelation, which provided a lens through which contemporary events were understood. One Fifth Monarchist leader justified their activism by quoting Daniel 7:18, "The saints of the most High shall *take* the kingdom" (King James Version; more recent translations translate "receive" rather than "take"). Another Fifth Monarchist wrote to Cromwell after they had parted ways with him, calling him the little horn of Daniel (Dan. 7:8) and the beast of Revelation. A leading Fifth Monarchist thinker used the numbers of days mentioned in Daniel 12 to predict Christ's appearance in 1701, though this date was not embraced by all of his comrades. He also offered a reading of the seven vials of wrath in Revelation 16 in which the first vial was Luther's reforms; the second, Parliament's abolition of episcopacy in 1646; and the third, the execution of Charles I and the troubles of other ungodly governments. Four vials remained to be poured out.

Although the Fifth Monarchists shared with other Christians the belief that the ritual laws of the Torah had been abolished by the coming of Christ, they looked forward to the restoration of biblical civil law, particularly the laws of debt, theft, sexual morality, and Sabbath observance. The concern for debt appears to be related to the social status of the majority of members of the movement. While a few were people of high standing – Thomas Harrison, the most illustrious, was a major general in the New Model Army, a member of Parliament, and one of the judges at the trial of Charles I – most were of more modest means, and many worked in the cloth and leather industries. The desire for Sabbath observance closer to that prescribed by the Torah was not uncommon among dissenters, some of whom favored returning the Christian Sabbath to the seventh day. On this question, the Fifth Monarchists were divided.

The restoration of the monarchy in 1660 dealt a severe blow to the hopes of the Fifth Monarchists, but many continued to believe that the new age was near. They saw the accession of Charles II as the last gasp of the old order and called for repentance on the theory that their own sins were to blame for the delay of the millennium. A few participated in Venner's Uprising, a short-lived and ineffective attempt to overthrow the government in 1661, just after the restoration, but while they embraced the idea that human beings could help to bring about the millennium, they largely avoided violence. Some understood the Great Plague of 1665–6 and the Great Fire that destroyed much of the center of London in 1666 as the beginning of God's destruction of the Antichrist, despite the death of many of the saints in these catastrophes.

Cromwell had been rather tolerant of the Fifth Monarchists, but the government of Charles II was far less so. Those closely associated with the execution of Charles I were put to death, and others were imprisoned. The new government also imposed censorship that made it difficult for the Fifth Monarchists to publish the pamphlets that had been their primary mode of propaganda. Yet despite persecution and defections as hopes for the eschaton dimmed, Fifth Monarchist churches can be traced through the 1670s and into the 1680s.

The Sabbatian Movement

The mid-1660s brought exciting news from the east to European millenarian circles: the appearance of a Jewish messiah apparently in the process of restoring his people to the Holy Land, an important step in the eschatological scenario to which many of these millenarians subscribed. The messiah was Shabbetai Zevi, born to a wealthy family in Smyrna (Ismir), in what is today Turkey, in 1626. From an early age Shabbetai Zevi called attention to himself by his strange behavior, which Gershom Scholem, the great twentieth-century scholar of Jewish mysticism, identified on the basis of contemporary descriptions as the effects of what we would today call bipolar syndrome.

In his mid-teens, Shabbetai Zevi left his teachers to study on his own and began to engage in ascetic practices associated with Kabbalah, the medieval Jewish mystical tradition. By the time he reached his twenties, he was going through periods during which he would perform acts that violated Jewish law, such as pronouncing the tetragrammaton, the four-letter personal name of God, and celebrating in a single week the three festivals associated with different moments in the agricultural cycle, Passover, the Feast of Weeks, and the Feast of Booths. During these periods he would claim that he was the messiah. Such periods were followed by periods of deep depression, which he understood as demonic attacks.

In 1665 Shabbetai Zevi decided to seek a cure for his mental afflictions by going to Gaza to consult a learned young kabbalist named Nathan who had gained a reputation for prophetic powers that enabled him to determine the root of each person's soul and reveal the proper kabbalistic rites to cure the soul of its ailments. But instead of providing a cure for his affliction, Nathan attempted to persuade Shabbetai Zevi on the basis of a vision he had seen that he, Shabbetai Zevi, was the messiah. The vision apparently reflected Nathan's previous awareness of Shabbetai Zevi and his strange behavior dating back some years earlier to a time when both men had lived in Jerusalem. In place of a cure Nathan offered a kabbalistic interpretation of Shabbetai Zevi's psychological instability as evidence of his messianic role: his inner struggles were a reflection of his battle against the forces of evil in order to rescue the divine sparks trapped within them, while the forbidden acts Shabbetai Zevi performed were a way of hallowing even the roots of evil. This daring interpretation reflects the thought of the great sixteenth-century kabbalist, Isaac Luria. According to Luria, the act of creation required the Godhead to contract into itself so as to provide space for the world to be created. But tragically the vessels created to hold the divine light in the space thus created were not able to fulfill their task; they broke, and some of the divine light was lost, scattered into the realm of darkness. When Jews perform the commandments enjoined by the Torah, they liberate these divine sparks from their imprisonment in the realm of evil. Luria's theory serves to explain why a world created by a good and omnipotent God is in need of redemption, and it had a profound impact on kabbalistic thought.

Nathan's persuasion finally prevailed. Late in the spring of 1665 in Gaza Shabbetai Zevi announced himself as the messiah. Jewish communities of the Ottoman empire were deeply divided over his claims, but his supporters included not only the poor and uneducated but rabbis and communal leaders as well. As the months passed, the excitement among Ottoman Jews grew, and word reached not only Christian millenarians, as already noted, but also the Jews of Europe, creating great excitement there too. While his impact on the course of history was certainly not comparable to that of Jesus, in his own lifetime Shabbetai Zevi was much more famous and had a far larger following.

At the end of December 1665 Shabbetai Zevi sailed from Smyrna for Istanbul, where he planned to take power from the sultan. The excitement had by then spread to Istanbul, and even Muslims were aware of the impending arrival of the Jewish messiah. He was arrested even before his boat reached the city and brought to trial. But although the Ottomans typically executed leaders of rebellions, Shabbetai Zevi was not put to death. Perhaps because this rebellion did not involve arms the grand vizier had Shabbetai Zevi imprisoned in rather comfortable quarters where he held court for his followers. But if the grand vizier had hoped that this lenient treatment would encourage the Jews of the Ottoman empire to return to life as usual he was disappointed. The excitement only increased during the months of Shabbetai Zevi's imprisonment. After some months the Ottoman authorities changed their approach, offering Shabbetai Zevi the choice of Islam or death. He chose Islam.

In the aftermath of Shabbetai Zevi's conversion most of his followers concluded that they had been mistaken in their hopes. But many were too deeply committed to give up on their messiah even in the face of such a devastating turn of events, and Nathan of Gaza was soon ready with an explanation. The apostasy was only the most dramatic expression of Shabbetai Zevi's struggle with evil from within, the most extreme of his strange acts. His conversion to Islam allowed him to enter into the heart of evil and to struggle with it from inside the realm, to redeem those sparks that had fallen too deep into evil for redemption by more standard means. It is possible that Shabbetai Zevi shared Nathan's understanding. In any case, he continued to practice many Jewish rituals even as he lived as a Muslim in the ten years that remained before his death at the age of 50. Some of Shabbetai Zevi's followers followed him into Islam in order to help in his mission while others, including Nathan, continued to live as Jews even as they held on to their belief in his messianic mission.

Even Shabbetai Zevi's death did not mean the end of this mission according to Nathan, who continued to explicate the meaning of his career until his own untimely death in 1680. Some Jews came to understand Shabbetai Zevi not as the final redeemer but as the messiah son of Joseph. Others believed that the messiah son of Joseph would have to come before Shabbetai Zevi could return, and there were a number of men who laid claim to that tragic role. Well into the eighteenth century Sabbatian believers could be found among even the most learned Jews of Europe and the Ottoman empire. In Turkey the descendants of Jews who had followed Shabbetai Zevi into Islam, known as the Dönmeh, retained a distinctive identity into the twentieth century.

Jacob Frank

In the mid-eighteenth century another messianic claimant emerged out of a Sabbatian milieu, Jacob Frank (1726–91), a charismatic Polish Jew who had close contact with Sabbatian groups in the Ottoman empire as well as Poland. In keeping with kabbalistic beliefs about the transmigration of souls, Frank claimed to be a reincarnation of the soul that had resided first in Shabbetai Zevi and then in Barukhiah, the founder of a Dönmeh sect that had influenced Frank at the beginning of his career. Overturning the law was a central principle of Frank's theology, and eventually he led his followers to convert to Christianity, which in Poland meant Catholicism, as a step to bring the messianic age closer, just as some of Shabbetai Zevi's followers had converted to Islam.

The Seventh-Day Adventists

While the Seventh-Day Adventists are not lineal descendants of the Fifth Monarchists, they emerged out of a similar Protestant milieu, though two centuries later and on the other side of the Atlantic, in which interpretation of the Bible was central to eschatological expectations. Western New York State in the nineteenth century was home to a variety of religious movements. It was there that Joseph Smith claimed to have discovered the gold tablets of the Book of Mormon in the late 1820s. There were a number of Shaker farms in the area, and in the middle of the century the Oneida Community was established there. The Seventh-Day Adventist movement grew out of the preaching of William Miller, a Baptist farmer who taught that the Second Coming would take place on October 22, 1844. Miller arrived at his prediction on the basis of his reading of Daniel 8:14, which prophesies 2,300 days until the cleansing of the sanctuary. On the assumption that each day of Daniel's prophecy equaled a year and that the period to which the prophecy referred began with the decree of Artaxerxes to rebuild Jerusalem in 457 BCE, Miller concluded that the year to which the prophecy referred was 1844. The prophecy's reference to the cleansing of the sanctuary meant that the Second Coming would take place on the biblical Day of Atonement, the seventh day of the tenth month of the calendar of the Torah. In 1844, according to Miller's calculations, this date fell on October 22.

Needless to say, Miller and his followers were disappointed in their hopes. Indeed, the failure of the Second Coming to take place on the date Miller had predicted came to be known as the Great Disappointment. But one follower, Hiram Edson, reported seeing a vision on the morning of the following day in which he learned that Miller was correct that October 22, 1844, was a crucial date in the eschatological timetable, but it was not the date on which Christ was to return to earth. Rather, it was the date on which Christ was to enter the heavenly holy of holies, just as the high priest had entered the holy of holies of the Jerusalem Temple every year on the Day of Atonement. The date marked the beginning of the cleansing of the cosmic sanctuary and thus the inauguration of an eschatological process that would become manifest on earth only in the future, though the near future.

Those of Miller's followers who embraced this revised eschatological scenario formed what came to be known as the Seventh-Day Adventist Church. The church was also distinguished by its insistence that Christians remained obligated to observe all of the Ten Commandments including a seventh-day Sabbath with the cessation of labor required by the Torah. Though the Seventh-Day Adventists may have gone farther than others in their embrace of the biblical Sabbath, as we saw in the discussion of the Fifth Monarchists, the English dissenting churches placed a high value on Sabbath observance, and some were even inclined toward observing it on the seventh day. Another defining feature of the Seventh-Day Adventist Church was its belief in prophecy as a living phenomenon. Its most important prophet, Ellen White, was active from the beginning of the movement until her death in 1915.

Despite their origins as a sect focused on the imminent end and their distinctive beliefs and Sabbath practices, Seventh-Day Adventists gradually moved closer to other evangelical Protestants, revising or downplaying aspects of their doctrine to reduce the gap. As White herself insisted, prophecy was subordinate to the words of the Bible. But at least in theory the imminence of the eschaton remained central to Adventist beliefs. This in combination with Adventist acceptance of prophecy made it possible, indeed likely, that new prophets would arise with more intense eschatological expectations.

One such prophet was Victor Houteff, who came to see himself as playing the roles of Elijah and John the Baptist in ushering in the end time. After a public refutation of his teachings by the Seventh-Day Adventist hierarchy in 1934, Houteff moved his followers from California to a site outside Waco near the later Mount Carmel center. This group came to be known as Davidian Seventh-Day Adventists. Houteff's death in 1955 led to a split among his followers. Benjamin Roden became the leader of the group that came to be known as Branch Davidians. Roden saw himself as the true Elijah who would succeed where Houteff had failed. Roden's group took its name from his identification of himself and his followers as the branch mentioned in several biblical prophecies. For many years Roden and his wife Lois worked to acquire land in Israel and to encourage Branch Davidians and other Seventh-Day Adventists to settle there in anticipation of the last days. But Roden also developed the center at Mount Carmel in Texas, and it was there that he had himself crowned as God's vice-regent on earth.

David Koresh and the Branch Davidians

Vernon Howell, the man who later took the name David Koresh, arrived at Mount Carmel in 1981. By this time Benjamin Roden was dead, and leadership of the movement had passed to Lois Roden. Howell was a high-school dropout from a dysfunctional family whose mother was a Seventh-Day Adventist. He was drawn to the church as a young man, but he was officially disfellowshipped after telling the pastor of the church he had joined in Tyler, Texas, that he had seen in a vision that he should marry the pastor's daughter.

Yet despite his lack of formal education and his difficulty in writing polished English, Howell developed a broad and detailed knowledge of the Bible. This knowledge enabled him to put forward an eschatological scenario deeply informed by the Bible as read in the Branch Davidian tradition but also quite innovative. Koresh interpreted the book of Revelation, the special focus of his interest, by reading it in light of other biblical books, particularly the prophets and Psalms, relating figures from Revelation to figures in other biblical works, which he understood in eschatological terms. Thus, for example, the royal figures of Psalms are not King David but the future Davidic king, who can thus be identified with figures from Revelation. Though they would hardly be persuasive to anyone outside the Branch Davidian tradition, Howell's readings, which he claimed had been revealed to him by God, are often quite ingenious.

By 1983 Howell's charisma and interpretive skill were evident to everyone at Mount Carmel, and with Lois Roden's support he began to preach to the community. Though Howell was in his early twenties and Roden in her mid-seventies, they became lovers. But despite the status Howell enjoyed while Roden was still the head of the community, once Roden stepped down, it was not Howell but George Roden, the Rodens' oldest son, who succeeded in establishing himself in her place. Howell left the community for Palestine, Texas, some distance from Mount Carmel, taking with him forty or fifty followers, a significant portion of the group. During this period he traveled, making converts and visiting Israel. He also started using the name David Koresh, which is fraught with messianic significance, as will be discussed shortly; he changed his name legally in 1990. In 1988 George Roden, whose mental illness produced extremely erratic behavior, lost control of the Mount Carmel community after a gun battle with Koresh and his followers led to his arrest.

One foundational element of the Branch Davidians' approach to the Bible is common to virtually all the apocalyptic movements discussed here: the belief that biblical prophecy is primarily concerned not with events of the past but with the group itself and its own time. As with many other Christian apocalyptic movements, including the Fifth Monarchists, the book of Revelation was central to David Koresh's eschatology. For Koresh it was evident that the evil empire of Revelation was the contemporary enemy of the righteous, the United States, which he saw as a corrupt and decadent society that stood ready to persecute him and his followers.

Koresh identified himself with several of the positive figures in Revelation: the Lamb (Rev. 5), the figure on the white horse (Rev. 6:2 and 19:11), and the seventh angel whose voice will be heard at the end of days (Rev. 10:1–7). Since the Lamb clearly represents Christ, Koresh's identification with it implies that he also saw himself as Christ. But the meaning of this claim is not entirely clear. Some of his followers suggest that Koresh believed that Jesus became Christ at the moment of his baptism when the Christ spirit came to him. Thus Koresh himself could become Christ because he had received the Christ spirit. On some occasions, however, Koresh appears to have spoken in the first person about events the gospels relate about the life of Jesus.

But whatever the details of his thinking about his relationship to Jesus, it is clear that Koresh understood himself as the most important eschatological figure prophesied by the Bible and as more than merely human. The name he chose for himself refers to two aspects of the messianic role he understood himself to play. The first name designates him the eschatological Davidic king. The last name is the Hebrew for Cyrus, the Persian king to whom the book of Isaiah refers to as God's anointed, his messiah, because he overthrew the Babylonian empire, permitting the exiled Israelites to return to their land.

Koresh's view of the United States as persecutor is rooted in Seventh-Day Adventist eschatology, which understood US laws establishing Sunday as a day of rest as persecution and identified the United States as the second, lamb-like, beast of Revelation 13. But Koresh himself had other reasons to fear the government of the United States, for he was engaging in behavior prohibited by its laws: sexual relations with underage girls and polygamy. Koresh explained his relationships with girls and unmarried women in the group as necessary to allow him to father the twenty-four children he understood as required by biblical prophecy to be princes of the world at the eschaton. In 1989 he went farther, telling his followers that God had commanded him to have sexual relations with even the married women in the group, while all other men in the community were to renounce sexual relations. Although a few members left Mount Carmel after hearing this new revelation, most accepted it. These arrangements put the group in constant danger of accusations of child abuse, sometimes from disgruntled one-time followers who had left Mount Carmel. Fear that the children at Mount Carmel were being abused was one of the main reasons the FBI was unwilling to back off when it became clear that it would be extremely difficult to remove the Branch Davidians from their compound.

The book of Revelation also provided Koresh with a timetable for the eschaton. He identified his own day as the time of the fifth seal (Rev. 6:9–11), when the souls of the martyrs were to take their place under the altar in heaven. Thus for Koresh the book of Revelation itself made it clear that he and his followers must expect persecution. But it also made it clear that the end was very near.

Even the end of Koresh's career on earth did not bring an end to the expectations of some of his followers. Because Koresh had predicted his own martyrdom, it was by no means impossible to fit the events at Mount Carmel into his eschatological scenario, and some continued to look forward to the unfolding of its last stages. Indeed, from one point of view, Koresh's claims about the fifth seal had been fulfilled: he and his followers had become martyrs, and their souls could now take their place under the heavenly altar. Some surviving members of the group, basing themselves on the book of Daniel, predicted that David Koresh would return in 1996 or 1999. But with the destruction of Mount Carmel the movement, which never numbered more than a thousand, shrank to perhaps a few hundred. The surviving Branch Davidians have not yet found a new leader, and perhaps never will.

Habad Hasidism

David Koresh was not the only messianic claimant in the United States in the 1990s. Indeed, although Menahem Mendel Schneerson (1902–94), the rebbe of the Habad or Lubavitcher Hasidim, never attracted the kind of attention that the Branch Davidians' confrontation with the FBI brought to David Koresh, he commanded a significantly larger following and left a more lasting legacy.

The Hasidic movement emerged in early eighteenth-century Poland around the figure of Israel Ba'al Shem Tov as a reaction against traditional eastern European Jewish culture, which viewed talmudic learning as the greatest religious attainment. Kabbalah too was central to this culture, but study of kabbalistic texts, which followed on mastery of the talmudic tradition, was restricted to the elite. The Hasidic teachers emphasized a more joyous and immediate religious experience and made kabbalistic traditions more accessible to ordinary Jews. As the students of the Ba'al Shem Tov established Hasidic communities across eastern Europe, they met with opposition from proponents of the traditional elite Jewish culture, known as Mitnagdim, "opponents." But as both groups faced the threat to traditional Jewish life posed by the forces of modernization, they grew closer together. In time Hasidism lost many of the features that had historically distinguished it from other forms of ultra-orthodox Judaism. For example, talmudic learning became central to Hasidic life. But one distinctive feature that remained was the role of the rebbe.

Each Hasidic community is centered on a rebbe, a charismatic holy man who is understood to mediate between God and his followers. His Hasidim look to the rebbe not only for spiritual guidance but also for advice on matters from marriage to business; his opinion is uniquely valuable because of his access to the divine sphere. Yet while the earliest rebbes were generally men of great spiritual gifts, over the years succession tended to pass from father to son or some other close relative so that genealogy came to replace charisma as the criterion for leadership. Thus dynasties sprang up with distinctive approaches to Hasidism, though in many cases after the early years the spiritual and intellectual quality of leadership was lower.

Habad Hasidism was founded in mid-eighteenth-century Lithuania, and its distinctive characteristic was its early integration of traditional talmudic study into Hasidism. The name Habad is an acronym of the Hebrew words for wisdom, knowledge, and understanding, which have kabbalistic significance but also point to the high value the movement placed on learning. The movement is also known as Lubavitcher Hasidism after the town in Russia where Shneur Zalman of Liadi, the first rebbe, grew up. The leadership of the community was not always passed on from father to son, but all seven men who served as rebbe were related. The seventh rebbe, the figure of greatest interest to us, was the son-in-law of the sixth rebbe and a descendant of the third rebbe, who was the great-grandfather of the sixth rebbe and whose name, Menahem Mendel Schneerson, the seventh rebbe also bore.

The sixth rebbe, Yosef Yizhaq Schneerson, led the movement through the most difficult years of the twentieth century. He was born in 1880, and when he became rebbe on his father's death in 1920, just after the Russian Revolution, he faced an unprecedented situation: as part of their larger campaign against religion, the Communists closed nearly all the Jewish schools and yeshivot in the Soviet Union. The rebbe tried to support traditional Jewish life, and in 1927 he was arrested and sentenced to death. But after international protests he was released and allowed to leave the country. He reestablished his court in Warsaw, where he stayed until 1940 and the arrival of the Nazis. He then fled to the United States; his youngest daughter and her family remained in Europe and died at the hands of the Nazis. Late in the war, as he began to understand the extent of the murder of Habad Hasidim and other traditional Jews of eastern Europe, Yosef Yizhaq came to interpret the awful events of the century as the travail that would precede the end, the birth pangs of the messiah. The sins of the Jewish people had caused the destruction of the Temple almost nineteen hundred years earlier, and the exile that followed had not yet brought them to repentance. Indeed the nineteenth and twentieth centuries were a time of unprecedented falling away from Judaism; fewer and fewer Jews remained loyal to the Torah. But now, as the Jewish people faced death, repentance was even more crucial than in previous generations since the messiah was more desperately needed than ever before. But World War II came to an end without the appearance of the messiah, while the establishment of the State of Israel in 1948, a cause for rejoicing elsewhere in the Jewish world, was for the rebbe and his followers a sacrilegious human usurpation of the messiah's role.

Menahem Mendel Schneerson

Redemption had still not come in 1950 when the sixth rebbe died without leaving clear instructions about a successor. Of his two surviving sons-in-law, the husband of the elder daughter seemed the obvious choice since he had been his father-in-law's close collaborator and was the head of the Habad yeshivah. But in the end it was the other son-in-law, Menahem Mendel Schneerson, who won out. From one point of view his victory is somewhat surprising. Although he had received a traditional education in his youth, Menahem Mendel had never studied at a yeshivah and had received a secular education in addition to his Jewish education. Later he studied at a university in Berlin and then, following the rise of Nazism, in Paris, before he and his wife went to America in 1941. But from another point of view it was precisely his education, irregular for a member of the rebbe's inner circle, that made him the right choice to lead Habad in its new home in America in radically new circumstances.

From the beginning of his time as rebbe Menahem Mendel continued his father-in-law's agitation for repentance to bring the messiah. He suggested that the arrival of Habad in America constituted part of the eschatological drama: now the Torah had come to the far reaches of the world to prepare the way for the messiah. Most important, he moved from the realm of theology to the realm of action. He sent out emissaries, married couples who settle in the community to which they are sent, to establish Habad's presence all over the world, from American university campuses to China, Nepal, and India. On campus they invite Jewish students, including those with no previous knowledge of Judaism, for meals, offer classes, and arrange religious services. In places where there are no established Jewish communities,

Habad houses provide Jewish travelers with religious services, kosher meals, and Passover seders. Gavriel and Rivka Holtzberg, a young couple murdered by terrorists in Mumbai in 2008, were engaged in just such work. Today the operation involves thousands of emissaries. Their goal is to encourage Jews to increase their religious observance and connection to Judaism. From the point of view of the Lurianic kabbalistic theology that undergirds Hasidism, the performance of divine commandments is important not only as an indication of repentance but as a way of reuniting the sparks lost in the cosmic catastrophe of creation with the Godhead so as to bring about the messianic era.

The seventh rebbe also oversaw a series of mitzvah campaigns, which continue to the present. (*Mitzvah* is the Hebrew and Yiddish word for "commandment.") The first, which he set in motion just before the Six Day War in an effort to secure divine protection for Israel, focused on tefillin (phylacteries): Habad Hasidim stood in public places and invited male Jewish passers-by to perform the commandment of binding on tefillin. Campaigns focusing on other commandments, such as Torah study, the lighting of Sabbath candles by women and girls, kashrut (the Jewish dietary laws), and giving charity, followed. There were also seasonal campaigns focusing on commandments related to a specific holiday, such as visiting a sukkah (booth) and waving the "four species" (the citron together with palm, myrtle, and willow branches) during the Feast of Booths and lighting candles during Hanukkah. In 1974 Habad introduced mitzvah tanks in New York City; by now the tanks are used elsewhere as well. These vans or recreational vehicles serve as mobile centers for the mitzvah campaigns, providing a convenient space into which passers-by can be invited for prayer and Torah study. During the Feast of Booths, the tanks carry a sukkah.

Through its emissaries and its campaigns Habad has achieved a public presence far beyond anything any other Hasidic or ultra-orthodox group has ever achieved or, indeed, has ever desired to achieve. Furthermore, while his predecessors could reach an audience beyond those in physical proximity to them only through their writings and word of mouth, as the first rebbe of the era of electronic communication, Schneerson was able to become a presence even for followers living in distant places in a way that none of his predecessors could have done. Radio and television allowed followers living far from Brooklyn, as well as anyone even casually interested, to experience the gatherings at which the seventh rebbe addressed his followers as they took place, while cassettes, and later CDs and DVDs, made it possible to hear and watch the rebbe's talks at any time. The rebbe did not live long enough to exploit the possibilities of the internet himself, but in the years since his death Habad has established a significant presence on the web at Chabad.org, with content that includes videos of some of the rebbe's talks, classes on a variety of subjects, the opportunity to engage in traditional study with a partner, and features directed at children such as KabbalaToons, cartoons with a spiritual message.

As the decades passed, Menahem Mendel's messianic language became stronger and stronger and the eschatological expectations of his followers grew more and more intense. By the 1970s the identification of the rebbe himself as the messiah had begun. I recall being fascinated and astonished when, sometime in the mid-1970s, a fellow graduate student, who had been a pupil at a Habad secondary school in Brooklyn, reported having heard the identification from some of the older Hasidim at a festive occasion after a few toasts had made them less careful in their choice of words. They explained, as Habad messianists would later say publicly, that the three consonants that make up the Hebrew word *mamash* (*m-m-sh*), an emphatic term meaning "actually," or "really," represented the initials of Menahem Mendel Schneerson. Thus, slogans claiming that the messiah was surely – *mamash* – coming soon pointed to the rebbe's messianic role. Since these slogans were coined by the rebbe himself, they offer some insight into the rebbe's own view of the matter.

But despite the implications of his program and the widespread acceptance of his messianic identity by his followers, Schneerson never clearly proclaimed himself the messiah. Instead he put forward a more traditional position: each generation contains someone worthy of being the messiah, but his ability to fulfill the role depends on the nature of the generation. Of course Schneerson's repeated insistence that his was the last generation and that redemption was on the verge of breaking forth, combined with his preeminent status in his movement, strongly implied that he was the messiah. But his position also provided an out if all did not go as planned: the rebbe was surely worthy, but his generation was not.

In 1992 the 90-year-old Schneerson suffered a stroke. This indication of human frailty did nothing to dampen the enthusiasm of his followers. Rather, it served to intensify it: redemption must be imminent indeed. Although Schneerson was never able to speak again, he did appear before his followers, and he is reported to have indicated acceptance, by waving the hand unaffected by the stroke, of their acclamation of him as King Messiah.

While his father-in-law lacked sons, Menahem Mendel himself lacked children altogether. Thus neither son nor son-in-law was available to succeed him. But despite the fact that he reached extreme old age in full possession of his faculties, Menahem Mendel never designated a successor, presumably because he expected to inaugurate the messianic age in his lifetime, making the question of succession irrelevant.

In 1994 Schneerson died. Some of his followers abandoned their expectation of imminent redemption: the rebbe was worthy, but obviously the generation was not. But others continued in their conviction that the rebbe was the messiah and would return from the dead to continue his work of redemption. Some went so far as to claim that Schneerson had not actually died but had only appeared to die. Even as the years passed and Schneerson failed to return to complete his mission, many Habad Hasidim remained convinced that he was the messiah. Even more remarkable, some messianists have developed what one might call a high Christology for the rebbe, in which he is addressed in prayers and associated with the Godhead. The parallels to Christianity were not lost on observers from the academy or even from within the world of traditional Judaism.

Major Habad institutions do not proclaim Schneerson as messiah, at least not to the outside world. Thus, for example, the website mentioned above, Chabad.org, does not make messianic claims for the rebbe. But the significance of this silence is by no means clear. It could indicate that those in charge of the institutions no longer believe that the rebbe is the messiah, but it might instead reflect caution in dealings with the outside world. On significant dates such as the anniversary of the rebbe's death full-page ads in the *New York Times* hail Schneerson as the living King Messiah; at least some Hasidim, then, remain convinced that the rebbe is the messiah and look forward to his manifestation as such. The failure of the movement to choose a successor so long after his death also points to the power of its messianic faction.

Apocalyptic Movements and Apocalypses

As we enter the twenty-first century, then, it is clear that the eschatological impulse that emerged among ancient Jews in the centuries before the turn of the era is still alive and well. For the Fifth Monarchists at the beginning of the modern era and the Branch Davidians at the end of the twentieth century and many Christian apocalyptic movements in between, the ancient books of Daniel and Revelation are foundational. It is surely significant that most Christian apocalyptic movements since the dawn of modernity have emerged out of Protestant churches with their embrace of the view that each individual can understand Scripture on his or her own. The Jewish messianism exemplified by the Sabbatians and Habad, on the other hand, is based less on Scripture than on Kabbalah, the Jewish mystical tradition that emerged in the thirteenth century, providing new avenues for eschatological speculation and expression alongside the eschatological scenario of *Sefer Zerubbabel* with its debt to Daniel and biblical prophecy.

As we have seen, the author of the book of Daniel, who chose to write under the name of an ancient hero because he believed that the days of direct prophecy were past, made his hero both an inspired interpreter of dreams and a recipient of angelic interpretation of Scripture. There is a certain irony in the fact that the book he composed came to be pored over and interpreted for its insights into the eschaton even as he himself pored over previous writings, including the book of Jeremiah and its prophecy of seventy years until the restoration of Israel (Daniel 9; Jeremiah 29).

There is perhaps even greater irony in the fact that the intense interest of modern readers in the book of Daniel is possible because its author was so wrong about the date of the end: the dates he predicted passed well over two millennia ago. But just as the author of Daniel was convinced that Jeremiah's prophecy of seventy years was not wrong but merely misunderstood, so too later readers were convinced that Daniel's prophecy was correct if only one knew how to read it.

The revelations of the apocalypses of antiquity were not limited to the coming of the new age. As we have seen, apocalypses involving ascent to heaven were less interested in the eschaton than in other types of secrets, including cosmological phenomena, the fate of souls after death, and the heavenly temple. But the apocalypses in which these interests were most clearly expressed, the Book of the Watchers and works indebted to it, did not become part of the canon (except in Ethiopia) and thus eventually their impact on Jewish and Christian tradition began to fade, though the tradition of tours of heaven and hell remained alive into the Middle Ages, and ascent to the heavenly temple remained a topic of interest through late antiquity in the hekhalot texts.

One of the most characteristic features of the apocalypses is the understanding that at least some exemplary human beings are the equals of the angels. This idea is a central theme of the ascents to heaven, which show their visionaries traversing the boundary and arriving in heaven, but it is also present in apocalypses focused on eschatology in which the visionary finds himself in conversation with angels who sometimes acknowledge him as an equal. It is an idea that stands in some tension with the dominant view in the Hebrew Bible that only trouble can result from human attempts to enter the divine sphere, and it is also fits poorly with the Christian understanding of Jesus as the one and only divine human being. Yet it is a powerfully attractive idea, and the apocalypses express it in a particularly powerful way.

It is also a very dangerous idea when it moves from the realm of the text to everyday life. While the apocalypses attribute more than human status to great heroes of the past, safely out of the way, many of the apocalyptic movements considered in this chapter attribute such status to their own leaders and sometimes even to their followers. As we have seen, the results are often disastrous. They make very evident the wisdom of the apocalypses' insistence that the arrival of the eschaton is the task of God, not of human beings, even human beings who have become the equals of the angels.

Further Reading

Translations of primary texts that are not part of the Bible or Apocrypha appear under the relevant chapter headings.

Introductions to the Early Apocalypses and the Pseudepigrapha

Collins, John J. *The Apocalyptic Imagination: An Introduction to the Jewish Matrix of Christianity*, 2nd edn. Grand Rapids, MI: William B. Eerdmans; Livonia, MI: Dove Booksellers, 1998.

Nickelsburg, George W. E. *Jewish Literature Between the Bible and the Mishnah: A Historical and Literary Introduction*, 2nd edn. Minneapolis: Fortress Press, 2005.

Chapter 1:   Scholarly Works Mentioned

de Jonge, Marinus. *The Testaments of the Twelve Patriarchs: A Study of their Text, Composition, and Origin*. Assen, Netherlands: Van Gorcum, 1953.

de Jonge, Marinus. *Studies on the Testaments of the Twelve Patriarchs: Text and Interpretation*. Leiden: Brill, 1975.

Kraft, Robert A. "The Pseudepigrapha in Christianity." In John C. Reeves, ed., *Tracing the Threads: Studies in the Vitality of Jewish Pseudepigrapha*. Atlanta: Scholars Press, 1994.

Milik, J. T. *The Books of Enoch: Aramaic Fragments of Qumrân Cave 4*. With the collaboration of Matthew Black. Oxford: Clarendon Press, 1976.

Chapter 2:   Book of the Watchers (1 Enoch 1–36)

Himmelfarb, Martha. *Ascent to Heaven in Jewish and Christian Apocalypses.* New York: Oxford University Press, 1993, chapter 1.

Nickelsburg, George W. E. *1 Enoch 1: A Commentary on the Book of 1 Enoch, Chapters 1–36; 81–108.* Hermeneia. Minneapolis: Fortress Press, 2001.

Nickelsburg, George W. E., and James C. VanderKam. *1 Enoch: A New Translation.* Minneapolis: Fortress Press, 2004.

Reed, Annette Yoshiko. "Heavenly Ascent, Angelic Descent, and the Transmission of Knowledge in 1 Enoch 6–16." In Ra'anan S. Boustan and Annette Yoshiko Reed, eds., *Heavenly Realms and Earthly Realities in Late Antique Religions.* Cambridge: Cambridge University Press, 2004.

Chapter 3:   Daniel

Collins, John J. *Daniel: A Commentary on the Book of Daniel.* Hermeneia. Minneapolis: Fortress Press, 1993. With an essay on "The Influence of Daniel on the New Testament" by Adela Yarbro Collins.

Nickelsburg, George W. E., and James C. VanderKam. *1 Enoch: A New Translation.* Minneapolis: Fortress Press, 2004. [translations of the Book of Dreams (1 Enoch 83–90) and Apocalypse of Weeks (1 Enoch 91, 93)].

Sparks, H. F. D., ed. *The Apocryphal Old Testament.* Oxford: Clarendon Press, 1984. [translation of 2 Baruch].

Chapter 4

The Dead Sea Scrolls

García Martínez, Florentino. *The Dead Sea Scrolls Translated: The Qumran Texts in English,* 2nd edn., trans. Wilfred G. E. Watson. Leiden: Brill; Grand Rapids, MI: William B. Eerdmans, 1996.

García Martínez, Florentino, and Julio Trebolle Barrera. *The People of the Dead Sea Scrolls,* trans. Wilfred G. E. Watson. Leiden: Brill, 1995.

4   Ezra

Stone, Michael Edward. *Fourth Ezra.* Hermeneia. Minneapolis: Fortress Press, 1990.

Parables of Enoch (1 Enoch 37–71)

Nickelsburg, George W. E. "Son of Man: 2. The Parables of Enoch." In David Noel Freedman, ed., *The Anchor Bible Dictionary*. New York: Doubleday, 1992.

Nickelsburg, George W. E., and James C. VanderKam. *1 Enoch: A New Translation*. Minneapolis: Fortress Press, 2004.

VanderKam, J. C. "The Righteous One, Messiah, Chosen One, and Son of Man in 1 Enoch 37–71." In James H. Charlesworth, ed., *The Messiah: Developments in Earliest Judaism and Christianity*. Minneapolis: Fortress Press, 1992.

2 Baruch

Sparks, H. F. D., ed. *The Apocryphal Old Testament*. Oxford: Clarendon Press, 1984. [translation].

Revelation

Barr, David L., ed. *Reading the Book of Revelation: A Resource for Students*. Leiden: Brill, 2004.

Chapter 5: Ascent Apocalypses

Himmelfarb, Martha. *Ascent to Heaven in Jewish and Christian Apocalypses*. New York: Oxford University Press, 1993.

Sparks, H. F. D., ed. *The Apocryphal Old Testament*. Oxford: Clarendon Press, 1984. [translations of 2 Enoch, Apocalypse of Abraham, Apocalypse of Zephaniah (Anonymous Apocalypse), Ascension of Isaiah, 3 Baruch].

Chapter 6

Tours of Hell and Paradise

Himmelfarb, Martha. *Tours of Hell: An Apocalyptic Form in Jewish and Christian Literature*. Philadelphia: University of Pennsylvania Press, 1983.

Schneemelcher, Wilhelm, ed. *New Testament Apocrypha, Revised Edition of the Collection Initiated by Edgar Hennecke*, vol. 2, trans. R. McL. Wilson. Cambridge: James C. Clarke; Louisville, KY: Westminster/John Knox, 1992. [translations of Apocalypse of Peter and Apocalypse of Paul].

Hekhalot Texts

Alexander, P. "3 (Hebrew Apocalypse of) Enoch." In James H. Charlesworth, ed., *The Old Testament Pseudepigrapha*, vol. 1. Garden City, NY: Doubleday, 1983. [translation].

Schäfer, Peter. *The Hidden and Manifest God: Some Major Themes in Early Jewish Mysticism*, trans. Aubrey Pomerance. Albany, NY: State University of New York Press, 1992.

Smith, Morton. "Hekhalot Rabbati: The Greater Treatise Concerning the Palaces of Heaven." With corrections by Gershom Scholem, transcribed and edited with notes by Don Karr. <http://www.digital-brilliance.com/kab/karr/HekRab/HekRab.pdf>, accessed July 5, 2009. [translation].

Swartz, Michael D. *Mystical Prayer in Ancient Judaism: An Analysis of Ma'aseh Merkavah*. Tübingen: Mohr (Siebeck), 1992. [includes translation].

There is as yet no English translation of *Hekhalot Zutarti*.

Chapter 7

Jewish Apocalypses of the Byzantine Era

Himmelfarb, Martha. "The Mother of the Messiah in the Talmud Yerushalmi and Sefer Zerubbabel." In Peter Schäfer, ed., *The Talmud Yerushalmi and Greco-Roman Culture*, vol. 3. Tübingen: Mohr Siebeck, 2002.

Himmelfarb, Martha. "*Sefer Eliyyahu*: Jewish Eschatology and Christian Jerusalem." In Kenneth G. Holum and Hayim Lapin, eds., *Shaping the Middle East 400–800 C. E.: Jews, Christians, and Muslims in an Age of Transition*. Bethesda, MD: University Press of Maryland, forthcoming.

Reeves, John C. *Trajectories in Near Eastern Apocalyptic: A Postrabbinic Jewish Apocalypse Reader*. Atlanta: Society of Biblical Literature, 2005. [translations of *Sefer Zerubbabel, Sefer Eliyyahu*, Secrets of Rabbi Simeon bar Yohai, Prayer of Rabbi Simeon bar Yohai, Signs of Rabbi Simeon bar Yohai].

Christian Apocalypses of the Byzantine Era

Alexander, Paul J. *The Byzantine Apocalyptic Tradition*, ed. Dorothy deF. Abrahamse. Berkeley: University of California Press, 1985. [includes translation of Apocalypse of Pseudo-Methodius].

Reinink, G. J. *Syriac Christianity under Late Sassanian and Early Islamic Rule.* Aldershot, UK: Ashgate/Variorum, 2005.

Chapter 8

Medieval and Early Modern Apocalyptic Movements

Cohn, Norman. *The Pursuit of the Millennium: Revolutionary Millenarians and Mystical Anarchists of the Middle Ages*, revised and expanded edn. New York: Oxford University Press, 1970.

The Fifth Monarchists

Capp, B. S. *The Fifth Monarchy Men: A Study in Seventeenth-Century English Millenarianism.* London: Faber & Faber, 1972.

The Sabbatian Movement

Idel, Moshe. "Saturn and Sabbatai Tzevi: A New Approach to Sabbatianism." In Peter Schäfer and Mark R. Cohen, eds., *Towards the Millennium: Messianic Expectations from the Bible to Waco.* Leiden: Brill, 1998.

Scholem, Gershom. *Sabbatai Sevi: The Mystical Messiah, 1626–1676*, trans. R. J. Zwi Werblowsky. Princeton: Princeton University Press, 1973.

The Branch Davidians

Newport, Kenneth G. C. *The Branch Davidians of Waco: The History and Beliefs of an Apocalyptic Sect.* Oxford: Oxford University Press, 2006.

Tabor, James D. "Patterns of the End: Textual Weaving from Qumran to Waco." In Peter Schäfer and Mark R. Cohen, eds., *Towards the Millennium: Messianic Expectations from the Bible to Waco.* Leiden: Brill, 1998.

Habad

Berger, David. *The Rebbe, the Messiah, and the Scandal of Orthodox Indifference.* London: Littman Library of Jewish Civilization, 2001.

Elior, Rachel. "The Lubavitch Messianic Resurgence: The Historical and Mystical Background 1939–1996." In Peter Schäfer and Mark R. Cohen, eds., *Towards the Millennium: Messianic Expectations from the Bible to Waco.* Leiden: Brill, 1998.

Friedman, Menachem. "Habad as Messianic Fundamentalism: From Local Particularism to Universal Jewish Mission." In Martin E. Marty and R. Scott Appleby, eds., *Accounting for Fundamentalisms: The Dynamic Character of Movements.* Chicago: University of Chicago Press, 1994.

Index

conquest by Persia 8, 40
Jewish exile in 7–8, 11, 26, 65
Bar Kokhba revolt (132–5) 117
Bar Koziba (bar Kokhba) 117
2 Baruch 6
and destruction of Second
Temple 55, 56
and dialogues 58
and eschatological timetable 44
and four kingdoms 62
and influence of Daniel 35
and messiah 68
3 Baruch 92–5
Christian elements 93
and destruction of Second
Temple 55, 92
and origins of evil 93, 95
and sacrifice 76–7
Slavonic translation 5, 93, 100
and wonders of nature 90,
93–4
Belial 51
Bockelson, Jan (John of Leyden)
140–1
Book of Dreams
and animal imagery 36–7
and determination of
history 36
and eschatological timetable 42
and eschatology 40
and Maccabean Revolt 46
Book of Jubilees 18
and angels 27
and calendar 20
and Qumran community 50
Book of the Watchers 2–3, 15–30,
45, 124, 159
and angels 27–8
and ascent to heaven 6, 15,
20–3, 30, 75, 76, 97, 159
authors 29–30

and calendar 18–20
date 3, 15, 31
descent of the watchers 16–18,
30, 76, 116
and Enoch as mediator between
humanity and angels 27–8,
115
and eschatological timetable 40
Ethiopic translation 15
and heavenly temple 3, 21–3,
27–8, 29, 75
and Last Judgment 24–5, 28–9,
30, 47
and origins of evil 16–18, 25,
29, 93
and secrets of nature 3, 26–7,
89, 90–1, 94
and sectarianism 28–9, 50
and Torah 29
Branch Davidians 7, 137, 148–51
United States seen as persecutor
150–1
Byzantine empire 6–7, 117–35
Christian eschatology 126–35
Jewish eschatology 117–26,
133–4
and Muslim conquest 127–35
and Persia 118–19, 124–5

Cairo Genizah, and hekhalot
texts 104
calendar
and Astronomical Book 19–20,
26, 91
and Book of the
Watchers 18–20, 26
and Torah 19, 50
Cave of Treasures 129
Celsus 109
chosen one, in Parables of
Enoch 64–5, 68, 70

Civil War, English 141
Cohn, Norman 139–40
creation, as revelation of God 26, 90, 91–2
Cromwell, Oliver, and Fifth Monarchists 141–3
Crusades, as apocalyptic movements 139–40
Cyrus, king of Persia 8, 40, 65, 150

danger and testing, in hekhalot texts 109–11
Daniel 31–48
  and Ancient Near Eastern myth 38–40
  animal imagery 36
  date 31, 32
  and determination of history 46
  and eschatology 2, 6, 7, 158–9
  and Fifth Monarchists 141–2, 158
  and four kingdoms 35–6, 38, 61, 127, 130, 141
  Greek version 32
  influence on later apocalyptic literature 6–7
  as interpreter 31–3, 44–5
  and life after death 47–8
  and Maccabean Revolt 2, 31, 33, 45–6, 47, 49
  and prophecy 44–5
  and Revelation 71
  and Sefer Zerubbabel 119, 158
  and seventy weeks of years 40–1
  and son of man figure 6, 37–8, 39, 62, 65
  and watchers 16

Dante Alighieri, *Divine Comedy* 6, 103
David, king of Israel, *see* king, Davidic
De Jonge, Marinus 4
Dead Sea Scrolls
  11QMelchizedek 43
  Apocryphon of Jeremiah 43–4
  and Book of Jubilees 50
  and calendar 20
  and Daniel 32
  and 1 Enoch 2–3, 15, 28–30, 50
  hymns and liturgy 112
  and marriage within priestly families 23
  and messiah figures 52, 123
  Rule of the Congregation 52
  and sectarianism 50–3, 54
  Songs of the Sabbath Sacrifice 76–7
  War Scroll 51–2
descent, in hekhalot texts 105–8, 111–13, 159
Deuteronomy, and Torah 9–11
Dome of the Rock 127, 132
Dönmeh sect 146
dreams, interpretation 24, 31–3, 44

Edson, Hiram 147
Eliashib (priest of Judah) 12–13
Elijah
  ascent to heaven 30, 124
  and Branch Davidians 148
  in *Sefer Zerubbabel* 120–1
emperor, last 132–4, 140
end of the world 1–2
Enoch
  as angel 78, 80, 115
  in Book of the Watchers: ascent to heaven 21–3, 30, 75, 76;

high priests
  consecration 77–8
  as descendants of
    Phinehas 49–50
  and 2 Enoch 77
Hildegard of Bingen 138
history, as determined 35–6,
    40–4, 46
Holtzberg, Gavriel and Rivka 155
Houteff, Victor 148
Howell, Vernon, *see* Koresh, David
hymns, hekhalot 112

Ignatius of Loyola 138
imagery
  animal 36–7
  Canaanite 39
interpretation
  and *pesher* 51
  prophecy as 13, 44–5
Isaiah (prophet) 21, 68
  and suffering servant figure 63,
    64, 122
Ishmael, Rabbi 105, 106–7, 111,
    113, 115
Islam
  and apocalyptic move-
    ments 139
  and Arab conquests 127–35
  and Shabbetai Zevi 145
Israel, kingdom
  Assyrian conquest 7, 123
  and Josephite messiah 123

Jeremiah (prophet) 27
  and seventy-year punishment
    period 8, 9, 40–1, 158–9
Jerusalem
  and Antiochus Epiphanes 34
  Babylonian conquest 7, 40
  Dome of the Rock 127, 132

and Last Judgment 24
under Muslim rule 119, 127,
    132
New 72, 84–5, 125
under Persian rule 12, 127
and presence of God 20–1
Roman destruction 55, 67, 117
Jesus Christ
  as exalted angel 86
  as Lamb 70, 71–2, 150
  as messiah figure 67, 69–72, 73
Jewish Revolt (66–70 CE) 54–5,
    117
Joachim of Fiore 138
Job (book) 26, 27, 90
John the Baptist 66
John Chrysostom 129
John of Leyden 140–1
John of Patmos 69–71, 73,
    83–5
Josephus, Flavius 14, 50, 53,
    66–7, 72, 139
Josiah, king of Judah 9–10
journey to the ends of the earth
    (Book of the Watchers) 23–7,
    30, 90, 97–8, 124
jubilee concept 43–4
Judah
  Babylonian conquest 7–8, 10
  and Davidic messiah 123
  Persian rule 11, 33
  return from exile 8–9, 40
Judea
  messiahs and prophets 66–7
  Ptolemaic rule 14, 15, 33
  Roman rule 53–5, 61, 66, 117
Julian the Apostate 118, 131–2
Justin Martyr 18

Kabbalah 143–4, 146, 152–3,
    155, 158